FOUND OBJECTS

FOUND OBJECTS

A STYLE AND SOURCE BOOK

By Joseph Ruggiero

INTRODUCTION BY SUZANNE SLESIN

Foreword by
MARIO BUATTA

Text by
CAROL COOPER GAREY

with photographs by
J. BARRY O'ROURKE

Clarkson N. Potter, Inc./Publishers
DISTRIBUTED BY CROWN PUBLISHERS, INC., NEW YORK

To my mother, who had the unique ability to make something wonderful from nothing and to my father who respected and enjoyed the gift of vision

Inquiries should be addressed to Clarkson N. Potter, Inc., One Park Avenue, New York, New York 10016

Printed in Japan by Toppan
Published simultaneously in Canada by
GENERAL PUBLISHING COMPANY LIMITED

Design by Margery Peters

Library of Congress Cataloging in Publication Data

Ruggiero, Joseph.
    Found objects. A style and source book.
    Includes index.
    1. Found objects (Art) in interior decoration.
I. Title.
NK2115.5.F68R83   1981   747′.9   80–27904
ISBN: 0–517-541475 (Crown)

10 9 8 7 6 5 4 3 2 1

First Edition

Photograph on page 205, reprinted from
Plant Hangers by Dona Z. Meilach,
copyright © 1977 by Dona Z. Meilach, by
permission of Crown Publishers, Inc.

Half title photograph by J. Barry O'Rourke

Frontispiece:
Objects found in nature are displayed as furniture and art on the patio of designer Michael Taylor's house overlooking the San Francisco Bay. A tree trunk and a slab of stone serve as a rugged outdoor table, accompanied by two carved-out tree trunks as seats. The huge sculptural form in the background is a piece of driftwood.

Acknowledgments

This book has been in the making almost all my life, but it might never have happened without the support of my wife, BARBARA, and my children, MEG, BETH, and JOE. They have lived with found objects, have helped me discover them, and have sometimes seen possibilities in them that might never have occurred to me. They believed in what I had to say and deserve my special thanks.

Many other people have helped me along the way. I am especially grateful to the designers who opened their homes to me and directed me to their friends and clients. I offer here their names and the page numbers on which their designs appear. My thanks, then:

■ to RON MANN and IVY ROSEQUIST, who achieve breathtaking effects with the simplest of natural materials. Their home in California introduced me to a world of new possibilities with found objects *(pages 56, left; 118; 127, left; 130–131; 134, right; 135, left; 139; 147, bottom; 150–158)*

■ to MICHAEL TAYLOR, whose use of natural found objects, muted tones, and textures has become the basis of a worldwide reputation *(pages ii; 2; 9, upper left, 132; 160–161)*

■ to JOHN DICKINSON, whose converted firehouse in San Francisco seems to have been created and stocked by divine inspiration rather than finder's luck *(pages xx–1; 125; 126, top; 143; 178)*

■ to WILLIAM GAYLORD, also of San Francisco, for devising ingenious designs with found objects by simply repositioning familiar household possessions *(pages 65; 66, top and bottom)*

■ to MIMI LONDON, a Los Angeles designer whose adaptations of found objects are an education in the potential of natural and man-made materials *(pages 5; 46–47; 56 right; 58; 131, bottom; 162–163; 164–165; 172)*

■ And to DIXIE MARQUIS, her partner, who is equally graced with the talent for creating wonderful interiors with simple things. Her house and designs also appear *(pages 48–49; 56, right; 126, bottom right; 128, top center; 138; 162–163; 164–165; 173)*

■ to SARINA and JOHN MASCHERONI, of New York City and East Hampton, trailblazers among New York designers in the use of found objects, who can see the magic in an old door or a broken clock used in a new way *(pages 10; 20; 33, top; 53, top right; 59, bottom; 69; 78; 84; 136; 144, top left and right, bottom left; 148, top left)*

■ to GEORGIA JOHNSTONE, for her skillful applications of discards from plant nurseries and bold use of construction materials *(pages xvi; 17; 23, top; 122)*

■ to WILLIAM GOLDSMITH, another East Coast innovator, whose furniture showroom in New York is a showcase for "found" designers *(pages 21; 145, bottom right; 146, bottom)*

■ to ROBERT PATINO and VINCENTE WOLF, whose use of skids as a coffee table in Elsa Peretti's apartment has remained a landmark in home design *(pages 26–27; 99, bottom left; 129, top center; 135, top)*

■ to ALBERT HADLEY, a legend among designers. His scraps of paper, jug wine bottles, and washed-up coconuts could only be elegant *(pages 62–63; 120, top; 126, bottom left; 128, bottom left)*

■ to RICHARD LOWELL NEAS, for table settings that make found objects into visual feasts *(pages 23, bottom right; 100, top right; 111)*

■ to ROBERT METZGER, who can bring an old iron or a plastic food container to a new level of sophistication *(pages 28; 120, bottom; 141, left; 145, top right)*

■ to JOHN SALADINO, whose designs can transform stones and fishing poles into strong decorative elements *(pages 64, 124)*

■ to ANN LeCONEY, who is not above mixing bottles and soap boxes with elegant traditional furnishings *(pages 30; 34–35; 37; 77; 83; 103, bottom left; 108)*

■ to ALEXANDRA STODDARD, who includes family mementos and objects found at dairies with antiques and brightly colored fabrics *(pages 41; 147, top)*

■ to ARTHUR FERBER, whose striking apartment is, by the designer's own description, "a sophisticated version of the street" *(pages 4, left; 11; 145, top left)*

■ to RICHARD MAURO, who uses an astonishing range of materials to make expansive and controversial seating *(pages 38; 42–45; 100, top left)*

■ to RICHARD HOLLEY *(pages 14; 142, top and bottom left)*; to BEVERLY JACOMINI *(page 117)*; to ROBERT MIGLIO and THOMAS WEBB *(pages 54–55; 129, bottom right; 131, top)*; to RICHARD CAMP and DAVID MURRAY *(pages 76, bottom; 80–81; 128, bottom right)*; to JAMES RUDDOCK *(page 15)*; to ANGELO DONGHIA *(page 129, top right)*; to WALDO FERNANDEZ *(pages 8, left; 9, top right; 98)*; to MARIE VALK and CHARLES DAMGA *(pages 40, right; 74)*; to WILLIAM HODGINS *(page 121)*; to FERRUCCIO TRITTA *(page 6, top right and bottom left)*. And special thanks to MARIO BUATTA, for his foreword, his unflagging support, and his potpourri *(pages viii; 135, bottom right)*.

Scores of other friends and associates provided material and inspiration for this book. I also am very grateful:

■ to artists BILL SHIELDS *(pages 57, 72, 92–93; 170)*; HUBERT

LONG (pages 29, bottom; 76, top; 178); BOB LEVERING (pages 53, bottom left and right; 128, top left; 144, bottom right); and MICHAEL KRIEGER (pages 50; 70; 128, top right; 129, top left, bottom right; 9, bottom left)

■ to art directors JOE CHAPMAN (pages 6, bottom right; 9, bottom left); RICHARD TRASK (pages x, 180, top left); and TONY PALADINO (page 59, top left); and to advertising executive THOM SWEENEY (page 52)

■ to the experts on plants and flowers—ELVIN McDONALD (pages 36, 97, 113, 114, 115); C. Z. GUEST (pages 106–107); KENNETH TURNER (page 73); and RENNY REYNOLDS (pages 94, 102); and to food expert ROBERT CARRIER (pages 168–169)

■ to entertainers BOBBY SHORT (page 82) and PHYLLIS DILLER (page 22)

■ to the photographers whose extraordinary talents are displayed throughout this book: J. BARRY O'ROURKE, for all his tireless efforts and so many photographs taken on weekends and holidays, and to his wife, Carol, for her help (pages 13; 24; 32); to CHRIS MEAD for his constant encouragement (pages 7; 8, right; 86; 90; 116); to FRANK KOLLEOGY, to RANDY O'ROURKE, RUDI KLINE, and BILL THURSTON, with special gratitude to JEFF HUNTER. Thanks, too, to photographers LARRY DALE GORDON (pages 60, bottom; 71; 159), STEVE PREZANT (page 16), and ED SUN (pages 60–61), who are represented by their found objects

■ to MARY EMMERLING for leading me to the right people and supporting me along the way

■ to my brother and sisters, for the knowledge and direction they have given me

■ to my agents GAYLE BENDEROFF and DEBORAH GELTMAN for their confidence and guidance when things got rough

■ to BETTY VAUGHN who believed it could be done and talked me through the early stages of development

■ to my editor and confidante NANCY NOVOGROD who supported the original idea, gave of herself, and helped make this grow into a book. To my publisher JANE WEST, and to MIKE FRAGNITO, PAM POLLACK, JODY HOTCHKISS, GEORGE OEHL, and everyone else at CLARKSON N. POTTER. Thanks, too, to MARGERY PETERS for her design

■ to CAROL COOPER GAREY for understanding the book and persevering to bring the copy to life; and to SUZANNE SLESIN for believing in found objects and putting their use in perspective

■ to DONNA MINUCCI who spent hours at the typewriter and MARY SHOFFNER for her research

■ to DONA GUIMARAES, DENISE OTIS, and PATRICIA CORBIN for their advice.

And to all those others who are part of that "found fraternity" for expressing their ideas and friendship.

JOSEPH RUGGIERO
January 1981

Contents

Foreword

The rooms I have always wanted to live in are filled with a rich variety of decorative objects—photographs, stacks of books, flowers, porcelains. The walls and tables are covered with possessions that speak of attachments, hobbies, a private sense of beauty. These rooms can be created by an interior designer, up to a point. The framework for the objects, the style of furniture, the mix of patterns and colors, can be selected by a designer, but the possessions that distinguish a room, make it an intimate expression of self, can be selected only by the person who lives there.

Found objects appeal to me because they offer the possibility and the material for this personal expression. If the shapes, colors, and textures are pleasing, if the objects are interpreted with imagination, they can go anywhere. As a designer, I would certainly encourage a client who wanted to try found objects to use them.

This book contains many spectacular examples of furniture and decorative accents created from found objects. Almost all of them are deceptively simple. Merely positioning a wooden crate in front of a sofa as a coffee table or placing a flower in a container that once held yogurt is not enough. A found object that is a successful design element reflects the mediation of the person who has conceived it for its new role. It has undergone alchemy, been plucked from its original use and transformed into gold.

The objects in this book deal a daring blow to the rigid dictates of style and value—the design imperatives that furniture and accessories must be of the same or complementary period and that cost is the only measure of worth. Found objects are invitations to flights of fancy. They challenge us to invent, to expand the borders of what are considered the proper components for an interior. Though governed by the same design principles as traditional furniture and decorative objects—proportion, color, texture, scale, and placement—found objects offer almost unimaginable freedom. They entice you to experiment, and only become of value once their appearance in a setting pleases you. They can be discarded or placed aside for future use. When you tire of a found object, you can replace it.

Found objects can be sleek and hard-edged or baroque and intricately detailed. You will see the range in this book. They allow the personal to take root and flourish in a roomful of store-bought or custom-made furniture. Each found object is the unique expression of its interpreter. It is as individual as you or I.

BY MARIO BUATTA

Mario Buatta is one of America's foremost interior designers.

One's personal possessions—books, family portraits, a box of letters—can become decorative objects when they are casually placed around a room.

J. BARRY O'ROURKE

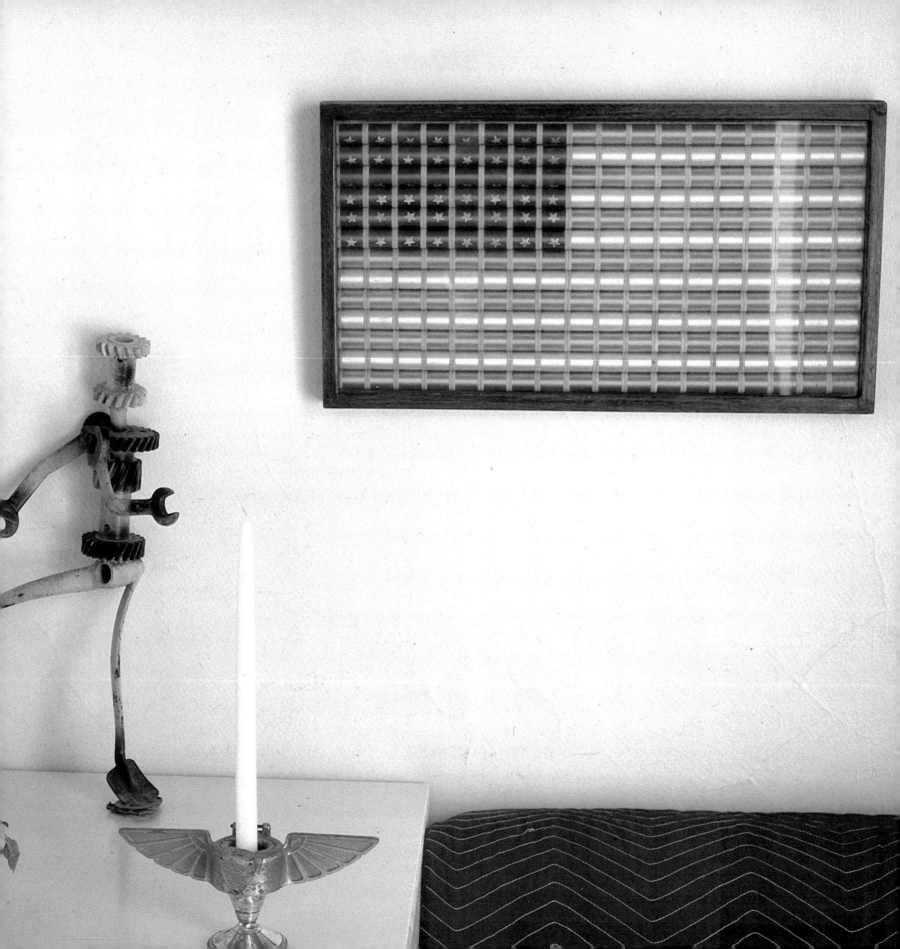

Introduction

There is something of the scavenger, the historian, the child, the archaeologist, the functionalist, the resourceful treasure hunter, the collector, the recycler, the poet, and the artist in us all—and finding an object and reusing it in our homes is a way to give expression to these facets of our personalities.

Some people prefer empty, serenely minimal rooms; others more cluttered environments, but the feathering of one's nest is an intensely personal endeavor.

Historically, the decoration of rooms was a way to display wealth and status. The highest degree of craftsmanship, the finest materials, the studied combination of objects, were all planned to emphasize the achievements, taste, and power of the person for whom the rooms were designed.

In France and England rooms were also used as settings for collections. These assortments of ornamental and occasionally utilitarian objects—sometimes costly, some-

Automotive spare parts have been arranged as a candlestand and sculpture. Spools that once held thread have been slid on dowels and painted like an American flag.

CHRIS MEAD

times of no monetary worth—expressed intellectual values and introduced an individual and eclectic note into the home.

By the late nineteenth century, with the development of an interest in the natural sciences, collections of butterflies, shells, and minerals were often on display, tangible clues to visitors that their host was a person of gentlemanly pursuits with a superior appreciation of the natural world. With the growing popularity of travel, objects carted back from faraway countries took their place among the collections. Travelers of that period found little of interest in things that we might now consider as fine art: African masks and tribal weavings, for example. Rather, it was unusual objects pertaining to the natural sciences that were held in high regard: seashells, tortoise carapaces, ostrich eggs, and elephant tusks. These souvenirs were placed in prominent positions where they might be admired by visitors.

Today, it is not only the curiosities of exotic natural beauty that appeal to collectors, and not only the ceremonial drums and the

carved statues that are valued by travelers; the more ordinary and unlikely objects are coming into their own. Such humble elements of the natural environment as tree trunks, driftwood, and rocks—once too commonplace to be noticed—are being discovered and put to use in the home. Their attraction is due in part to the fact that they have all but disappeared from the urban landscape.

Our interest in the conservation of the environment has hastened the inclusion of these objects in our living spaces, as nostalgic symbols for the places we feel we are in danger of losing. Instead of coveting these materials for their rarity, we are displaying and using them, along with many different things from nature, to create atmosphere.

We are not limited to the natural world in our reclamation of found objects. We are also rediscovering discarded man-made materials and packaging. We are spurred by a new recognition of the durability and design quality of such materials as paper, rubber, cardboard boxes, wooden crates, tin cans, bottles. Industrial remnants, as well, are being seen in a new light. Pieces of pipe, overscaled spools, construction elements, and the anonymously designed but simply shaped and unadorned equipment of the commercial world are finding aesthetic and functional uses in the modern interior. Buildings, too, once not considered suitable as dwellings, are being transformed into homes. No longer is it unusual to live in a house or apartment that a few years ago would have been considered bohemian or uninhabitable. Indeed, warehouses and factories, churches, banks, barns, chicken coops, and garages have been reclaimed from previous use and made into comfortable and inviting living environments.

In recycling these remnants of our twentieth-century society, we are signaling our acceptance of a new need to be resourceful. The cost of acquiring fine antique furnishings, and well-made modern goods has steadily risen, and the cost of new building has become prohibitive—so we are looking elsewhere. And we are developing a new "eye."

In the twentieth century artists were the first to celebrate found objects. This appreciation has been based as much on the recognition of their design possibilities as on the need for new materials. Their work and their vision have become the inspiration for myriad aspects of the modern sensibility in decorating and design.

During the first decades of this century, the Cubists were experimenting with collage, starting with a fragment of newspaper, a metro ticket, a shred of advertising memorabilia, a strip of wallpaper. These recognizable bits, borrowed from everyday life, were integrated into deceptively simple arrangements. Transformed, they somehow remained the same, taking on a timeless quality.

The Dadaists and Surrealists brought to the fore the whole question of the found object. In the catalog of the exhibition "Dada, Surrealism, and Their Heritage" (The Museum of Modern Art, 1967), William S. Rubin explained: "The Surrealist object was essentially a three-dimensional collage of 'found' articles that were chosen for their poetic meaning rather than their possible visual value."

It is now too easy to forget the surprise that greeted the works of the Surrealist and Dada artists, whose idea, of course, was precisely to stun and provoke the viewer. Artists like Meret Oppenheim, Man Ray, Marcel Duchamp, and Max Ernst borrowed ordinary odds and ends and used them in their artwork; clocks and teacups, bicycle parts, and household appliances figure in their pieces.

The Dadaists glorified the found object by drawing attention to it and they managed to play with its expressive qualities, its power to shock when placed out of context, its ability to puzzle, to disorient.

Meret Oppenheim's 1936 "Fur-Covered Cup, Saucer and Spoon" and Man Ray's "Flatiron with Metal Tacks," created in 1921, are two examples of the transformation of banal objects into powerful art images. Marcel Duchamp stuck a bicycle wheel onto a stool, adopted a commercial bottle rack, and entered a standard ceramic urinal, which he signed "R. Mutt!," into a major art exhibition. His "Readymades" were meant as a rebuttal of art itself. Ironically, today they are among the most widely copied and influential pieces of modern art.

Pablo Picasso offered the clearest example of an artist adapting and transforming the material at hand; he opened our eyes to objects we might have previously ignored. A toy car became a baboon's face, a bicycle seat and handlebars were changed into the head and antlers of his 1943 "Bull's Head."

In the 1950s and 1960s the imagery of found objects fueled a whole generation of American artists. Materials found in the trash or used in the studio were appropriated into the artworks, becoming both medium and message for paintings and sculpture.

Jasper Johns' flags and paintbrushes, Robert Rauschenberg's stuffed goat with a tire around its waist, the comic strip inspiration of Roy Lichtenstein, the use of photography and advertising from Pop culture in the works of Andy Warhol, George Segal's plaster castings of real people in real environments were examples of the use of new materials and subjects in art.

In the early 1960s Alexander Calder transformed slivered coffee and beer cans into a series of plumed cocks. The printed, multicolor cans became the gloriously colored plumage of free-flying birds.

In the same decade Gregory Turpan, a New York artist, constructed three-dimensional assemblages of such hardware store and warehouse items as streetcleaners' brushes, restaurant serving pans, plastic bottles, floor mats, janitorial buckets, and rubber plumbers' plungers. Ten years later, he disassembled his pieces and used the elements again in his home.

The range of fantastic worlds that rise phoenixlike from the remains of throwaway and rejected bits is a powerful example of the creative potential of the found object.

Simon Rodea's intricately engineered Watts Towers in Los Angeles are an extraordinary tribute to the magical possibilities of recycling. Almost entirely built of bits of household china, tile, Coke bottles, and metal scraps implanted into cement, and completed in the early 1950s, they create an otherworldly environment from the most ordinary of fragments.

The sculpture of Louise Nevelson, whose work incorporates bits of wood—some banisters, knobs, planks, newel-posts—is another example of the evocative possibilities in the use of found materials.

They are adopted for their shape yet become transformed by the artist until they are nearly unrecognizable. Covered in paint, they are an essential part of Nevelson's sophisticated and monumental pieces. More than random scraps of wood, they are the entryways to mysterious worlds.

Joseph Cornell's famous boxes are filled with recognizable and carefully chosen objects—clockfaces and dolls, corks and glasses, eggs and bubble pipes, maps and photographs. But they have a fascination and a mystery all their own.

"It is ordinary to love the marvelous; it is marvelous to love the ordinary," wrote Donald Windham, a friend of Cornell's. "For Cornell, the paradox was more complicated. He found the marvelous and the ordinary interchangeable. Objects were sometimes one, sometimes the other; and his inspiration came from this interchangeability."

"All decorating is found objects," insists Terence Conran, the author and home design expert. And, indeed, furnishing one's home is a matter of making choices.

Our tools for such a task are the objects around us. They can be nostalgic or devoid of sentimentality, purely functional or merely decorative. They can come from the natural or the industrial world, they can be rare and valuable or commonplace and cherished.

The process of selection is no longer restricted to department

stores or furniture showrooms. But using tree trunks or shells, tin cans, packing crates, or metal tubing is a slightly different activity, one which reflects how interior design sensibilities have changed.

The contemporary interior designer has become an artist himself, juggling styles and tastes, mixing the precious antique with the less exalted commercial remnant. The dramatic play of light, the reliance on large surfaces of color, the creation of a theatrical ambiance, a set tableau, are all interior design approaches that have sources in the art world.

The contemporary designer uses banal objects whose beauty might be unseen by others as a way of demonstrating his interests and creativity. Freed from the tyranny of a single style, he borrows from all of them, and explores sources other than artisan workshops.

The found objects he chooses not only represent different perceptions but symbolize different schools of design. The table base made out of a tree trunk is very much the natural California style; the flue pipe used as an umbrella stand emerges from the high-tech aesthetics.

As artists and designers make choices on visual grounds and apply their own personal preferences to the types of objects they select, the boundaries of the accepted broaden.

Gene Moore, the display director at Tiffany & Co. for the last twenty-five years, garnered a large public following by creating miniature windows—tiny spaces that are used to display jewels in unusual settings. "I showed people how beautiful dirt could be," he is fond of saying. Balsa wood, mechanical toys, ice-cream cones, or brown paper bags would pop up as props for rare jewels, fine crystal, bone china. The modest settings were endearing and surprising. They offered ideas, they captivated, they involved passersby.

Many of the best uses of found objects are simply responses to specific and often mundane design problems—a place to store all the children's toys, an inexpensive yet elegant dining table, a home for an ever-growing collection of matchbooks or work gloves. From supermarket cartons to abandoned farm equipment, there is something new to be made of anything that catches one's eye.

But the style of found objects changes, because one not only recalls the past but comments on it. In the 1950s, along with grasscloth walls and paper lampshades, the modernistic interior sported a cardboard egg-crate ceiling; that was one way the savvy designer proved that he was appreciating the shape of functional things.

In the late 1970s the architectural artifact signaled the modern and post-modern interior. There are the salvaged remnants of past decorative splendor—the egg and dart molding, the columned fireplace, the elaborate wood paneling, as well as the frankly theatrical and faked pastiche of the classical past—column, gargoyle, arch. These elements are tangible proof that one can nod approval at the classics, yet still have one's feet firmly planted in the present.

Found objects offer not only avenues of self-expression but true design and economic alternatives. They encourage people to look at shape and color, and free them from the constraints of the strict interior design styles.

One is alternatively surprised at how well objects of completely dissimilar natures subtly coexist—how a metal water trough can serve as a cocktail table in a luxuriously appointed living room—or at how winning an unexpected and surprising element is when it dominates a room.

In decorating, it is in the juxtaposition of the precious and the poor, the found and the chosen, the planned and the accidental, the timely and the timeless that one experiences a magical effect.

BY SUZANNE SLESIN

Suzanne Slesin is assistant editor of the Home Section of the New York Times *and coauthor, with Joan Kron, of* High-Tech.

The Art of Discovery

If you've ever happened upon a forlorn object that seemed to invite itself home, that pleaded for a second chance, that refused to be ignored, you've been overcome by the urge to scavenge. And if you've perceived that thing, not for what it was but for what it could be, you have known what it is to let your imagination roam. Artists and children are notorious scavengers. They look at rubble and rusty parts with a fresh pair of eyes, investigating the curious shapes, visualizing something far more wonderful than a lifeless log or a weather-beaten tin can. Once home, the log might be a doorstop, the tin can a table base. Found objects appeal to the artist and child in all of us; what may appear worthless may also be irresistible.

"Every means is right when it serves its end," said modernist artist Kurt Schwitters, who began using junk in his paintings in the 1920s. In an attempt to explain his rummaging through wastebaskets,

Discarded pipes, found near the construction site of a condominium, are stood on end as planters. Designed for outdoor use, the pipes stand on steps in the garden of the designer's home.

attics, and junk piles for collage materials, Schwitters announced, "I saw no reason that old trinkets, pieces of driftwood, checkroom numbers, pieces of wire and wheels, buttons, and rubbish could not be used as material for paintings on an equal footing with pigments manufactured in factories." By taking advantage of the unexpected, he put secondhand materials in new perspective.

Where to look for found objects? Ocean beaches, riverfronts, and lakesides produce a steady supply of materials redeemed from nature. Shells, stones, rocks, and pieces of driftwood will probably be worn smooth by the effects of water and time. Nature has a way of polishing the objects found on its shores. If you travel to tropical parts of the world, your pickings are likely to expand to include exotic fragments of coral and giant conch shells.

Less romantic perhaps, but easily accessible, are the urban locations—city streets, vacant lots, highways, and construction sites—where man-made debris is plentiful. Here is where you will find industrial equipment, abandoned containers, gloves, bits of wire,

chunks of cement. The highway is a treasure trove of leftovers, some mangled beyond recognition but interesting nonetheless. City streets are receptacles for all manner of rejects begging to be carted away.

Back in your own home, reevaluate the everyday things you might ordinarily discard—bottles, cans, cardboard boxes, and grocery baskets. Spare parts from broken tools, pieces of wood, and unused pipes may appear to be useless clutter in the basement; fabric scraps and forgotten things relegated to the attic. These are a few of the resources you can call upon. As you examine the objects, think of them in new contexts—as ornaments or alternatives to conventional furnishings—somewhat like a case of mistaken identity. For example, a tin juice can without its labels could be mistaken for a silver vase, a hollowed-out log for a plant stand.

Think of using the ordinary things around you in new ways. Some of the most exciting found objects are as accessible as your closet or your attic. The shirts or pants you might decide to hang on pegs on your wall or the gloves you might wish to tie up like a bouquet of languorous flowers become found objects when you discover a new place for them. They merely have to be repositioned to be found.

Depending upon how far your imagination will stretch, familiar objects can be something other than what they appear. If you have trouble visualizing a broken tool as anything but a broken tool, ask for a child's opinion. Chances are, you may gain new respect for the spare part, see it as a plaything, a primitive art form, or an unconventional piece of decoration.

It would be helpful to think in terms of objects from nature as being distinctly different from those that are man-made. Natural materials, such as rough bark, rocks, and shells, blend with the landscape; they are organic forms. As such, they often impart an outdoor quality to a room setting and resemble pieces of sculpture when standing alone. Man-made objects, such as metal fragments, tend to corrode and rust to the point where they appear ancient. The patina of age simply adds to their charm. No alteration is necessary to make them compatible with authentic antiques.

As found objects add to a room, they are also transformed by it. The rugged texture of natural materials and the simple lines of commercial packaging and industrial products undergo a transformation when combined with conventional furnishings. Found objects announce themselves as different, yet take on the cast of their surroundings—

they become at once more noticeable and more civilized. A rubber tire coffee table will be a dramatic accent to upholstery fabrics, and there is a good chance too that the fabrics will make the tires look like carved and lacquered wood.

When mixing found objects with traditional or contemporary furnishings, the fundamentals of design come into play. Color, scale, and texture dictate usage. If the object is small and rugged looking, it will mix easily in a traditional room; conversely, a smoothly textured man-made object, such as a tinted glass bottle, will work in a contemporary room. "Subtlety and wit are essential to this concept," suggests designer Albert Hadley. "There is a fine and delicate balance between worthless junk and a found object transformed into a decorative object for the home: the proper scale, the proper color, and the proper setting must all be considered." Since the eye is the best judge of what you like, you will learn by experimenting.

While many of the photographs in this book focus on professionals in the field of art and design, found objects are the universal decorative tools. There is no special technique for taking the object from where it was found and transforming it into a form of decoration; there are no elaborate instructions for building, finishing, or piecing together. Most found objects require minimal transformation: colors of woods can be left the way they were found, the patina of age unaltered. The

most you may need to do is nail something together or to a wall; wash off excess dirt, being careful not to remove its signs of wear. Much like folk art, found objects are naïve and appealing in their natural state.

Disposability is another feature inherent in found objects. Since they are free for the finding, they can be readily changed or replaced with no concern for their fragility. Rather than being returned to litter, the objects can simply be moved about or put away for another time, another place.

Most of the found objects that can be easily changed are small things—they are often random discoveries that can be carted home or stored away casually, without much effort or planning. Their transformation into useful or ornamental objects for the home is also casual. Such designers as Michael Taylor, Mimi London, and Richard Mauro are using their special skills to create important furniture with found objects. While many examples of their work are included, the emphasis of this book is on small things or simple things that one can do oneself.

The range of possibilities is enormous. Found objects can be used indoors and outside as elements of design or as bits of amusement; they can be furniture such as chairs or tables. They can be added pieces of decoration, storage units, wall ornaments, centerpieces, conversation pieces. They can be, simply, anything you want them to be.

Following pages: Coral branches, discovered by interior designer John Dickinson while vacationing in the tropics, are gathered in an ironstone vase in the center of the studio of his home, a converted firehouse. In the background, poised on matching columns, are papier-mâché heads—formerly used as display props—retrieved from a department store trash pile.

Objects in Place

CHAPTER ONE

TABLES

They organize our lives, stand ready to receive coffee cups, hold reading matter, display possessions. They are indispensable, but not necessarily conventional. Like people, some of the most interesting tables are thoroughly original, different in shape and size—and, at times, eccentric looking.

Tables can be heirlooms, custom designs, or mass-produced contemporary pieces. They can be major investments or they can simply be found, and therefore free. The former requires wherewithal, the latter ingenuity—and a sense of humor. "A cedar stump used for a table is one of a kind," says naturalist designer Michael Taylor. "You can't copy it or find the mate." Taylor, a pioneer in decorating with found objects, creates indoor landscapes using river rocks and boul-

Boulders, *the height of cocktail tables, serve as functional objects in Ralph Lauren's desertlike showroom. Like chunks of abstract sculpture, the rocks suggest art forms but are actually found tables with generous amounts of room on their surfaces for potted plants and accessories. The mottled colorings of the rocks blend into the neutral tones of the room.*

ders as rugged substitutes for commercially designed tables.

Among the first designers to give legitimacy to the found object as a table were Robert Patino and Vincente Wolf, whose pursuit of new design ideas lured them to remote regions of the world. They confirmed that necessity is, indeed, the mother of invention. "The farther one gets from civilized areas, the more people make do with what they have," says Patino, citing a South Seas custom of wrapping offerings in leaves rather than storebought gift paper. The partners' resourcefulness often leads to discovery. While refurbishing jewelry designer Elsa Peretti's apartment, they were stalemated when it came time to decide on tables. Conventional designs were ruled unfit. A stroll on Peretti's terrace solved their problem: it was there they found wooden skids with a collection of plants on top. The skids appeared to have the appropriate dimensions for the low-scaled furniture that would surround them. The only way to judge was to place

them near the sofa as makeshift cocktail tables. "We cleaned them off, sent for some bleaching solution, and brought them inside," says Patino. When the client sat down, propped her feet on the newfound table, she responded, "This is it!"

In order to qualify as a table, the found object should be an appropriate height to substitute for a conventional table, depending upon your personal requirements. Maryland designer Robert Sherman, who is always on the lookout for recyclable objects, found a creative solution for a room in need of a countertop to serve as a bar. An old wooden ironing board proved to be an ideal portable bar.

For a found object to act the part of a table, creative thinking is required on your part. Artist Robert Indiana discovered that when he stacked an even number of short railroad ties in square formation, he had fabricated a table for his studio in Vinalhaven, Maine. A piece of drawing board suffices for a tabletop. The common wooden crate, turned upside down, will certainly serve as a table next to a rustic chair indoors and out. An old sled can function as a low table next to a grouping of floor pillows in a lounge area of a ski house. A round washtub, filled with dried flowers, or a matchbook collection covered with a circle of glass could also be considered a table—and a conversation piece.

Tables need not be stationary, particularly if they are found objects. Considering the earliest portable tabletop was an animal skin that nomads spread on the ground, the table, as such, is open for interpretation. The sturdiest, least expensive picnic and lap tables can be fashioned from simple slabs of wood or an overturned shallow crate.

Apart from their obvious functions, tables can also contribute a boost of color to a given area. "All the found tables in my apartment act as color spots in the rooms as well as adding sculptural interest," says designer Ferruccio Tritta, who discovered new uses for acid green cans found on the streets of New York. The four cans have been put to work as cylindrical bases under a glass-topped cocktail table. If you are attempting to match a fabric or a multicolored rug, you might try to find cans in several different colors in your travels.

To achieve harmony among the traditional tables in your life and those that fall into the category of found objects, think of the latter as carefully chosen punctuation marks. Use them sparingly and with meaning. One unconventional piece may be all a room needs to lift its spirit.

Stump of wood, *topped by glass, makes a substantial table. The found object adds to the mix of rich textures created by the sisal rug, the rattan chair, and the carved wood candlestand.*

J. BARRY O'ROURKE

J. BARRY O'ROURKE

Stack of magazines *serves as a night table. A functional and colorful arrangement, the table changes with reading tastes.*

Door, perched on four rusted old cans *found in the cellar, is a serviceable table. Constructed without benefit of nails or glue, the table can easily be moved and assembled in different areas of the room. A wooden crate holds an attractive assortment of fruits.*

5

Cardboard shipping forms, *used to encase lamps, are reused as low tables next to floor pillows. A surprisingly sturdy composition of plastic-coated cardboard, the packing form can be turned upside down to hold books, plants, and a variety of odds and ends.*

Gas cans, *spotted on a New York City street, seemed a made-to-order base for a cocktail table. Their acid green color and bulky shapes are among the room's bold elements. Other large cans might also be used.*

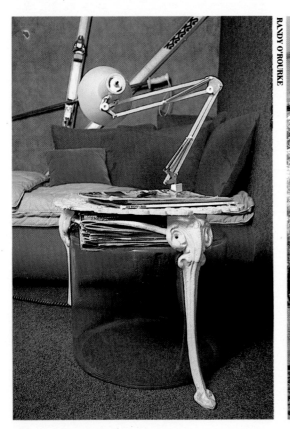

A broken garden table, *also found on the streets, has been propped up as an end table. Painted bright yellow—another primary color in the room—the found table, with only two legs intact, is supported by a cylindrical container.*

Adhesive cans, *found at a construction site, were the perfect match for this kilim rug. Supporting a glass tabletop, the cans contrast with shocks of color from the flowering quince and azalea.*

Terra-cotta flue pipes, *more commonly used as building materials, have aesthetic potential as tables. Here two matching square pipes support a larger rectangular tube and together serve as a holder for books and magazines. The clay surface, sturdy and easy to maintain, is a relative of the terra-cotta pot. Building a larger system simply requires additional pipes.*

Log with a slice removed *for firewood has enough surface expanse to accommodate a light repast. The log's interior grain matches that of the hardwood floor in this country house. An unconventional end table such as this is easy to come by and needs no alterations other than a coat of flat varnish to preserve its natural surface.*

Twigs joined with rawhide, *overlapping at the corner log-cabin fashion, originally served as a planter. With the addition of a sheet of glass, the construction made an unusual cocktail table.*

Indented boulder *was placed in a room next to a woven straw chair and columns of lacy bark. The boulder provides an interesting texture and serves as an ashtray holder.*

Three-tiered log table base *is a square formation of matched logs fastened at right angles and bound around the triple layers with braided rope. Log layers can be added or subtracted, depending on the desired height. Whittled log edges add to the handcrafted character. This particular table was fitted with a lacquered tray top; a square piece of glass would serve the same purpose.*

Log washed up by the Hudson River *was resuscitated to serve as a bedside table. A perfect bridge between woodlands and elegant furnishings, the table stands in a glass-enclosed country house.*

Tea-box tables, *with stenciling and metal edges as apparent marks of origin, look very much at home in a chintz-filled library. The boxes were rescued from a local tea company as they were about to be broken up for firewood.*

Metal paint can, *stored in the cellar, was reconsidered as an end table when new wicker furniture was installed. It proved to be the ideal size, and it adds a sparkle of color to the room.*

Two steel cylinders, *abandoned at a construction site, were retrieved to serve as bases for tables. Fitted with smoked glass tops, the soot-black objects adhere to the monotone scheme, their proportions in harmony with the low-scaled furnishings.*

Garbage can, *turned upside down, is a care-free end table in an informal family room. It is a childproof, low-maintenance piece of furniture that stands at a comfortable height next to the sofa and is roomy enough to hold a lamp.*

12

Collection of beer cans, *recycled into a Pop Art table, appears in the sitting area of a country kitchen. The cans were stacked and attached with metal glue to form a cube of columns. A square of clear acrylic was placed across the top (glass could be used as well). Circular or triangular configurations can also be formed from columns of cans, their labels providing a graphic display.*

J. BARRY O'ROURKE

Animal feeding trough *is now a stately cocktail table in a Texas apartment. An oval piece of slate conforms to the shape of the steel base; the large plant urn repeats the ridged design and carries it up into the room.*

Sewer pipes *support a glass tabletop in a New York apartment. The pipes were painted stark white to complement the bleached wood floor, their cylindrical forms alluding to modern architecture. The table succeeds in several practical uses: as a game table, desk, and dining table for six.*

Spool table *painted with white enamel, one of three in this photography studio, is set on casters. The table is used as a desk, for dining, or as a prop for photographs, and can easily be moved from one function to the next.*

Cardboard sonotubes, *molds for cement, are treasures to be sought from a friend in the construction business. Indentations at table height hold a neon-colored lucite board that serves as a desk or tabletop.*

17

CHAPTER TWO
TABLE SETTINGS

Setting a table is akin to preparing a meal: it can be a creative experience if you dare to be adventurous. An imaginatively designed table acts as a prelude to dining, a stimulant for the senses.

In certain tropical countries, the scooped-out shells of coconut, pineapple, and pumpkin serve as both bowls for food and table decoration. In Hawaii leaves are customary food wrappings; in Mexico cornhusks are traditional food servers and festive decorations. In all cultures, the table is a gathering place where the celebration of eating reflects age-old customs. The manner in which a table is set may be as diverse as the languages spoken during dinner. Table settings, like fashion, relate to the mood and manners of society. In the twelfth century, banquet revelers shared goblets and ate from communal platters with their hands. At the

coronation party for King James II, guests were seated at enormous tables on which hundreds of platters provided the decoration.

Table manners, it seems, have come full circle—from thoroughly relaxed to rigid and back to a convivial attitude that typifies our brunch and buffet styles today. The table setting is, after all, an invitation to relax, whether we eat with our fingers or with prescribed utensils. The elements of decoration—china, silver, glassware, and table covering—establish a mood, the centerpiece a focal point.

The center of the table is a perfect stage for found objects and for a display of creativity. Designer Ron Mann spreads the whole center portion of his dining table with beach glass (the smooth, small pieces of glass will not damage the finish of the table); tiny bottles with cut flowers are perched on the glass fragments. Shells and pebbles could be used in the same manner to create the illusion of a miniature rock garden. A center grouping of African violets or any brightly col-

ored flower in terra-cotta pots can be set off against a field of gray beige beach stones. To protect the finish on a wood table, or to guard against scratches on glass, a layer of cloth or plastic can be spread under the natural covering.

The changing seasons inspire many table-setting ideas. Advertising executive Doris Shaw collects a variety of objects she finds in country backyards and fields. Among her favorite possessions are perfectly formed bird's nests filled with china and glass eggs that she places in the center of the table. In summer she surrounds the nests with beach shells, in fall she makes a bed of vivid autumn leaves, and in winter she arranges bird feathers or curved branches around the nests. When not in use, her cache of objects is preserved in a closet.

Dried leaves arranged in mounds can also provide nesting places for name cards. Photo stylist Emilie Tolley gathers the smallest branches from her backyard, saving them for dinner parties. In addition to the leaves, she uses the

Split logs *support an assortment of breads in a richly grained wood ski house designed by architect Robert Venturi. Masses of food can be assembled and served on these giant logs, part of a winter's supply of firewood.*

sinuous branches as supports for place cards.

Setting the mood for a harvest party, caterer Martha Stewart arranged a large circle of cabbage leaves on a five-foot-round buffet table covered with a rust-colored cloth. One large candle stood on top of the leaves, surrounded by gourds, pumpkins, pomegranates, squash, and papaya. The edible decorations proved doubly useful, since they were incorporated in the menu of a subsequent meal. For another buffet party—this one an outdoor event—she covered a forty-foot-long rented table with brown wrapping paper—on top of which she spread peat moss. Piles of harvest vegetables, looking as if they had grown on the spot, encircled the platters of party food. For an alfresco seafood party, she substituted sand, shells, and coral for the harvest spread.

In addition to the table creating a mood or a specific theme, it can provide a surprise and an unexpected change of scenery. One hostess set a formal dinner table only to deliver the first course in Big Mac hamburger boxes. To her guests' amazement, the boxes contained curried shrimp in glass dishes, not the fast food they anticipated.

Mundane household objects may be surprise elements if used inventively. Colanders in three different sizes filled with fruits or vegetables can be clustered as a centerpiece. Muffin tins will hold a substantial supply of condiments for a curry party. A fluted mold can be filled

with water, a single backyard flower floating on top. As an alternative to a conventional tablecloth, an old gray army blanket can make an interesting covering for a table set with contemporary ceramic dishes and a center arrangement of pottery bowls holding votive candles.

Using a cheese flat as a centerpiece, Elvin McDonald turns mealtime into a horticultural event. After filling the wooden container with potted plants of unusual species, he mists the foliage and offers each guest a magnifying glass to observe the life within the tiny droplets of water that have formed on the assembled plants.

The dining table has been the scene of colorful events in every culture since man first refined the art of food presentation. What appeals to the eye whets the appetite. A wonderful-looking table is destined to do both.

J. BARRY O'ROURKE

Wire carrier for milk bottles, *dating from an earlier time, holds the makings for a portable cocktail party, with snacks in one section, wine and an assortment of beverages in the other. A container of olives—the original can used as a server—fits securely in one corner, cushioned by towel-wrapped breadsticks and crackers. Sprigs of dried flowers are tucked in a container between bottles and hors d'oeuvres.*

Overturned iron skillet *is used as a stand for candles. A crystal ball in the center reflects the flames. The tapestry-covered dinner table supports other household finds, such as the tops of Madeleine cookie boxes as coasters, shells as plate liners, and a flowerpot as a wine cooler.*

21

Artichoke nestled in a head of broccoli *is a festive centerpiece for a Christmas meal for two. The artichoke has been carved out to hold a candle, its underside pierced with toothpicks and secured to the broccoli.*

Plastic plant flat, *which once held plastic pots of flowers, has been converted to a tray for refreshments. The design of the flat mimics the trellises of the porch. The trays can be stacked for easy storage when not in use.*

Terra-cotta flowerpot *converts easily to bread holder with the simple addition of a napkin. This tall pot accommodates long loaves; a shallow version could contain rolls or fruit.*

Kitchen utensils overflow from a pan *as a table ornament in a country home. A warmer for instant coffee and soup serves as a wine coaster, assorted gadgets and molds spill onto the table, an old ice-cube tray—missing its center portion—holds bread. Scalloped newspaper is used as a table cover.*

Clay-flowerpot saucers *serve as holders for relishes and condiments, newspaper clippings of daily stock market figures as place mats, and film cases as salt and pepper shakers, on a cable-spool table.*

Tin-can servers *for sugar and cream resemble modern design pieces, though they were originally supermarket cans for cat food and fruit. The tops are removed with an electric can opener so that the edges are uniformly smooth. A handwrought spout was fashioned by squeezing the sides of the soft tin can now posing as a creamer. An old hubcap acts as a bowl for fruit. A metal hanger holds toast.*

Cat-food cans and margarine tubs *hold bonsai plants and soup as if they were originally designed for that purpose. The simple white tubs, devoid of pattern, resemble china and are ideal for delicate-looking appetizers garnished with bits of greenery and for individual servings of rice accompanying an oriental meal.*

Inverted nursery flat, *compliments of a local florist, originated as a crate for potted plants. Now a lap table, it holds an informal lunch for one.*

Rubber gloves, *once destined for the trash, were retrieved as holders for dining utensils. The gloves rest on a wooden board supported by buckets, which serves as a table for this alfresco breakfast. Coffee is poured from a crockery cordial pot positioned near a vase filled with beach weeds gathered en route to the water. All the food and equipment for breakfast can be transported in wooden crates that do double duty as seats.*

Split-leaf philodendron leaves *are used as place mats on a table decorated with pale lilac flowers—long stalks of agapanthus. The flowers may be preserved for several dinners, but the leaf mats will only remain fresh for one meal.*

Egg carton *is used as a server for deviled eggs and vegetable sticks. The clothlike place mats are actually paper cut from shopping bags previously used to carry swatches from fabric showrooms; pastry tins hold salt and pepper, strawberries nestle in their original boxes, and wine wrapped in linen towels rests in an old milk carrier.*

Styrofoam® packing material, *which once protected a stereo, performs anew. Its recessed compartments organize a light meal for one. The featherweight tray can easily be wiped off with a damp cloth for reuse.*

Stick construction *by artist Hubert Long whose imaginative objects are built, according to one description, "with all the seeming careless perfection of a bird's nest." This, Gaudiesque in its elaborate lines, is an assembly of twigs on a carved-out log base. Knowing his affection for natural materials, friends deposit piles of hand-picked twigs collected from a nearby beach in Long's backyard. The napkin rings were made from the limbs of a dried cactus. His work is exhibited at the Andrew Crispo Gallery, New York City.*

Rosewater bottles, *more commonly found in powder rooms and gourmet kitchens, are centerpieces on a dining-room table. The bottles, with their flowers in tones of the labels, repeat their owner's favorite color and are favors that guests may take home.*

Tin-can centerpieces *imitate the luster of real silver and fool the eye at first glance. Mixed with sterling flatware and Ruggiero family china, the cans take on the refinement of their surroundings. The ridged containers, varied in size, are filled with pachysandra, bittersweet, and chrysanthemums. In order for the cans to shine like mock silver, every vestige of label and glue has been removed. On the same table, flip tops from soda cans are bent to hold place cards. Paper clips, bent back so that the center portion turns upward, also support cards. Another familiar object in a new context: black flower vases that are actually plastic film cases.*

Large paint can, filled with tubes of photographers's paper, *is a decoration on a lunch table in a photography studio. The table—a plain pine board resting on two sawhorses—holds other found objects: the inner circles from roles of transparent tape for use as napkin rings; deli takeout dishes for use as clear plates at each place setting; juice cans as containers for celery sticks.*

Muffin tin *serves as a candleholder on an informal dining table in a farmhouse living room. The table, an old wood door now standing on two sawhorses, was discovered in a barn on the property. The recessed areas of the door act as organizers for place settings.*

Circle of grapevines, *wrapped at intervals with cord, functions as a centerpiece and a natural serving deck for nuts balanced around the top ridges. A plain wreath is adornment in itself, but embellished with nuts and fruit it is a fanciful serving platter. Wooden plates are the only other rustic tone on this sleek glass tabletop.*

Tomato paste, sauce, and puree cans *with bright red labels look as crisp and fresh as the produce they contain. This New York kitchen is stocked with a variety of cans and tins that move to the table as serving pieces.*

Wooden cheese crate table garden *was arranged as a centerpiece. The garden commands a major portion of the circular table, yet it allows guests to talk through the fine sprays of flowers. Sprigs of lipstick vine lie across the table and twirl around napkins. A baking-powder tin holds celery stalks and a striped bed sheet serves as a tablecloth.*

Floral wallpaper samples *are place mats on a breakfast table. Packets of sugar and boxes of cereal add color. The bright blue label on the bottle of mineral water complements the pastel tones in this Manhattan skyscraper.*

CHAPTER THREE
SEATING

Madame Récamier repaired to her gilt-edged mahogany lounge, Whistler's mother to her modest chair and wooden footstool. Languorous women in high-waisted gowns reclined on their chaise longues; white-wigged men posed on their richly upholstered fauteuils.

Each historical period reflects a certain manner of living and adornment. If one piece of furniture could convey the posture of a particular era, the chair would undoubtedly be it. Chairs are extensions of our personality; they make a statement about our social life. No matter what their heritage, chairs, like good friends, provide comfort and support.

California designer Mimi London attributes the recent proliferation of casual seating to a desire to escape from a stressful world and to return to the simple comforts of a favorite chair. Her handcrafted seating pieces rely on found objects for their basic shapes and familiar textures. Scavenged pieces of tree trunks, logs, and gracefully curved tree limbs provide the frames.

Says London, "We examine the pieces of wood and then determine if they will become chairs, lounges, sofas, or perhaps beds. The natural objects, as they are found, suggest what shape a seat will take. "You shouldn't use seating as a perch," she claims, "but as a nest."

Richard Mauro, a furniture designer who has experimented with found objects ranging from safety pins to floor sweepings and fabric scraps, has elevated the chair to an art form. Mauro describes his materials as "common and everyday things, used unconsciously by us all." Revitalizing industrial wastes, Mauro calls attention to the odds and ends we take for granted. His rubbish-filled pillow designs, not intended to be serious art, explore the alternatives to preconceived notions about seating. Found objects are, after all, alternatives to traditional seating. As such, they add individualism to a room that might otherwise be lacking it.

Alternative seating could also be fashioned from a wooden door resting on six matched portions of tree trunks or heavy logs on either end with two as center supports. The platform would have to be fastened to the bases with nails. A single mattress or several large cushions could cover the seating area. If the unit were placed against a wall, additional cushions might be lined up as backrests. Another found object that might be used for seating is the inflated rubber tube. You would need two pairs of tires, stacked side by side. The tires can be tied together with braided rope woven around the sides and through the center holes. Once the holes are stuffed with fabric remnants or other soft material (to keep seats level), a cushion can be cut to fit the diameter of the tubes.

Large and small wooden crates, turned upside down, make excellent seating platforms that can substitute for costly sofas. Position one large crate along a wall; fit a small-

Paperback chair, *by Richard Mauro, consists of five hundred soft-cover books within cargo netting. The loungelike creation is appropriately placed next to bookshelves.*

39

er crate into the corner so that it intersects the large one at right angles. Add more units, depending on the length you require. This arrangement will resemble a built-in banquette. The surface can be fitted with upholstered cushions, or the entire unit—top and sides—carpeted to match the floor.

As for chair coverings, old clothing offers interesting possibilities. California artist John Holmes makes caricatures of stools using worn sneakers, socks, and discarded sweaters as their upholstery. The legs of his stools wear cushioned socks with sneakers attached to the feet; seat cushions are covered with old sweaters. Dressed in this fashion, the seat poses as whimsical art.

The found object doubling as a chair is an improvisational piece of furniture and is meant to be used as an accent to whatever else is in the room. That one chair that bears your mark of individuality is a commentary on the times.

Lame chair *was considered useless until given a second chance as functional art. Rescued from the street, the abbreviated chair rests on an accommodating windowsill covered in draped fabric.*

Wooden display stand, *once a grocery-market prop for baskets of fruits and vegetables, is now a sofa in a family room. The end table was formerly a platform that fit into the stand. A bushel basket serves as a cocktail table.*

Milk cans, *no longer used by the dairy, were redeemed to serve as stools. Stationed around a confined seating area, the brass-colored stools are perfect seating for a room where ordinary chairs might be too bulky.*

RANDY O'ROURKE

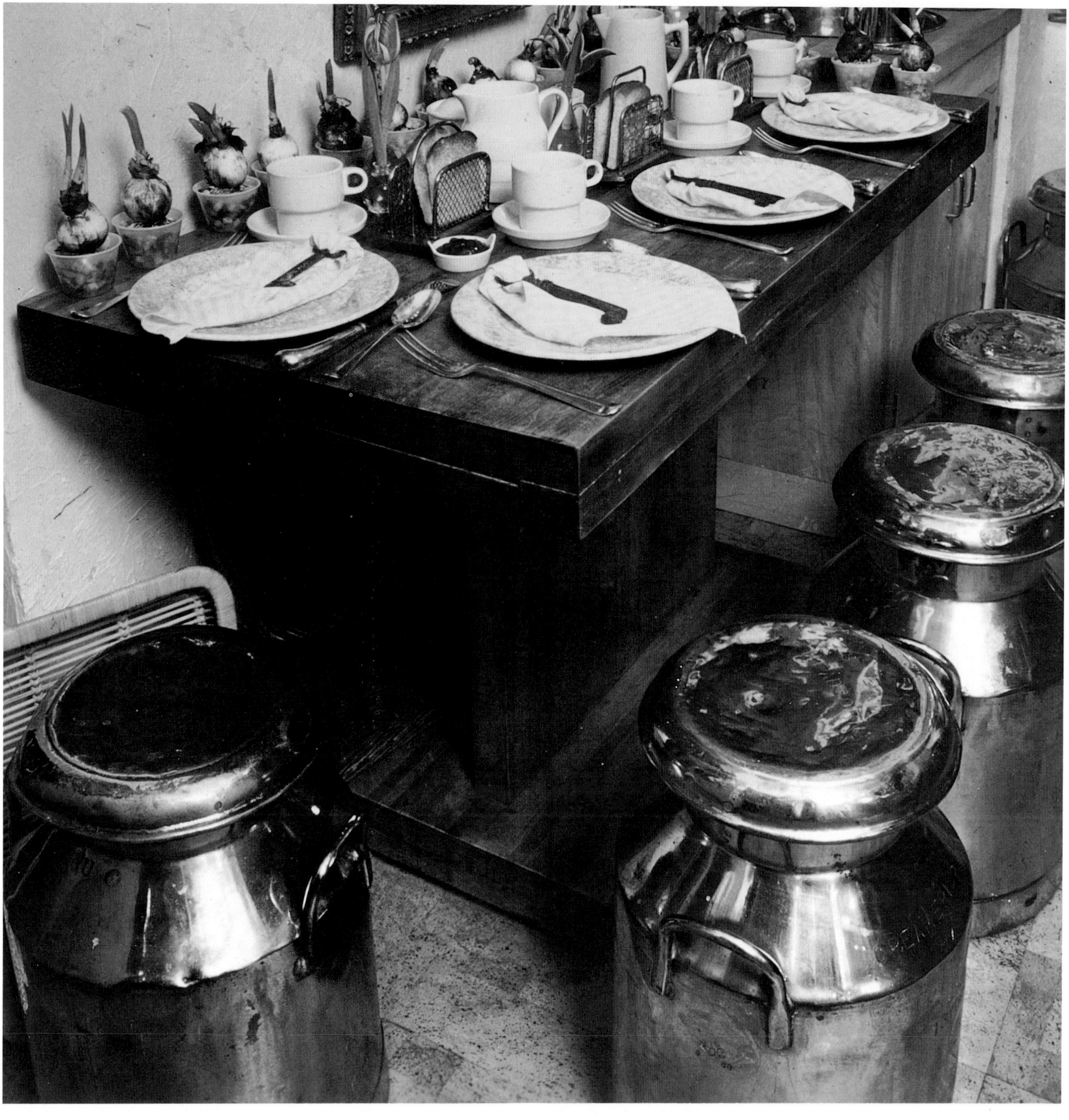

Resting places for discarded materials, *the work of Richard Mauro, comprise an accumulation of ordinary things with more artistic value than comfort. Mocking things we take for granted, Mauro experiments with such seating pieces as the safety-pin pillow, baby-bottle-nipple mat (for reclining), button cushion, newspaper ottoman, zipper chair. In the center, his Discus.*

Broken plates, *stuffed into a quilted canvas bag covered with aluminized nylon, form Mauro's Discus. The plates continue to break as people sit on them, although the canvas bag prevents sharp edges from poking through.*

Zipper chair *measures 45 by 36 inches high and has 150 yards of number 7 mesh aluminum teeth concentrically sewn on vinyl. Discarded zipper clippings are used as stuffing.*

Coil-spring chair *dedicated to Samuel Pratt, who patented the industrial spring in 1828. Mauro collected 150 pounds of assorted springs and used clear upholstery vinyl to shape the curious seat. Leftover coils frame the chair like welt stitching.*

Rag chairs, *Mauro's response to the litter problem, contain textile wastes, used paper cups, and assorted sweepings from New York streets. Wrapped in upholstery vinyl, the rubbish recalls gaily colored rag rugs.*

Parachute ottoman, *made of surplus army material with synthetic foam core. The fabric, wrapped around a 39- by 16-inch-high pillow, imitates the form of a parachute before landing, another example of Mauro's sleight of hand.*

Oil drums *were recycled by Mauro into chairs by carving out their center portions and lowering the lids to seat level. A coat of black lacquer restored their original gloss.*

45

Broken limbs of a cherry tree, *which was destroyed during a storm, were transformed into seating. After the branches were bolted together to form frames, the bark was sprayed with an acrylic preservative. The design of the armchair at left and the chaise longue at right was inspired by configurations of a tree the owner used to climb as a child in her grandmother's yard. Twigs are crisscrossed as a window covering in the room at right.*

Birch tree *suggested the shape of this chair. The branches were nailed together in their natural state and curved twigs secured to the frame to provide a backrest that supports a furry cushion—a squirrel's skin.*

Tree trunks *of a sophisticated nature. Like mushrooms, their shapes look as if nature intended them to be stools. The bleached stumps are capped with suede.*

49

CHAPTER FOUR

FOR WALLS AND WINDOWS

Ever since cavemen used walls for drawings of animals and landscapes, they have been surfaces on which to express oneself. Walls ensure privacy, and conversely they offer public spaces for displays of creativity. Apart from being a support system for roofs and ceilings, walls are inviting expanses much like empty drawing boards or blank pieces of paper that wait for composition. Once the composition has been created, a wall tells something about the people living within its confines.

One wall of artist Carol Anthony's cottage speaks of her affection for found objects. She has covered it with remnants: a three-dimensional collage of tattered dungaree shorts, stuffed animals, worn gloves, ballet slippers from childhood, hotel keys, vintage greeting cards. They are all tokens of her

Stiff shirt, *belonging to artist Michael Krieger, who dipped it in liquid starch and left it to dry on white canvas. Before positioning the old shirt, he spread glue on the canvas to create a permanent bond. The wrinkles impart texture, and the mounted shirt adds an unusual accent to the room.*

scavenging instinct and her findings.

Designer Albert Hadley reserves one wall in his studio for a display of found objects that have sentimental value. Coated with a sheet of cork, the wall resembles the page of a large scrapbook filled with magazine clippings, postcards, and fragments of notepaper with favorite quotations. The tapestry of mementos is ever-changing, postcards being replaced, clippings being removed to make space for other clippings.

Actor Jack Albertson appointed a wall in his Hollywood home as backdrop for an array of hats representing characters he has portrayed, each hat symbolizing another dimension of his career.

In all these instances, the full surface of the wall is used for the display of sentimental objects; the uncovered spaces between memorabilia act as a frame for each element on display. But most walls get by with only a few simple objects rather than an extensive collage. If the wall is large, it is well suited for

brightly patterned ornaments such as a collection of department store shopping bags or a bird-feed bag hung flat like a poster. One impressive found object can be as effective as a costly piece of artwork.

Instead of hanging an original painting on the solid white wall of her office, Mrs. Brooke Astor chose to display a souvenir of an exhibit at the Metropolitan Museum of Art's garden court: a piece of packing crate used to transport sod from China. Framed as if it were a painting, the object serves as a remembrance of her involvement with the exhibit.

Found objects such as a stack of old books or a pile of logs can also be used as sculptural elements at the base of a wall, adding texture and dimension to an otherwise smooth surface. A single piece of driftwood or a gracefully shaped branch can be hung on walls that have no other distinguishing features. A section of dune fence tacked above a sofa or mantel becomes a natural wood mural; an old straw hat, a musical instrument, a piece of clothing, can also be used for ornament.

Designer Angelo Donghia transformed one naked wall of his Key West beach house into a display area for colorful pieces of clothing; hats, gloves, capes, and jackets hang from plain wooden pegs in the style reminiscent of simple Shaker interiors. Donghia, whose home is judiciously accented with found objects, has this point of view: "Obviously I don't want to surround myself with junk, with flotsam picked up for no other reason than the whim of the moment, but neither do I want the overly serious, the self-conscious artistic statement. There's no point in simply displaying a prestige object if it is unconnected with your own experiences and emotions."

Objects that are sometimes referred to as "street art"—discarded forms such as misshapen workmen's gloves, crushed bicycle baskets, discarded hubcaps, and chrome automotive parts are also within the realm of wall art. And even such commonplace items as plain brown paper bags can be hung up. Display them, as designer Arthur Ferber does, like soft cubbyholes, bottoms attached to the wall with several pieces of double-sided tape. Using bags that are free from wrinkles, hang them horizontally with the open end facing into the room. If the bags are fresh, they will remain open, forming a series of square pockets on the wall.

A page from a glossy magazine folded into a fan would be an arresting decoration for a deeply colored lacquered wall. Paper labels from cans and bottles mounted in plastic frames become colorful graphics for kitchen walls; olive oil tins, flattened and nailed or glued to squares of weathered wood, become a handsome mural.

The wall itself can be considered a found object. In the San Francisco firehouse of designer John Dickinson, the original stone gray walls remain in their weathered condition, the cracks and peelings a reminder of the building's historic past. Even though the structure has been refurbished, the aged walls have not been tampered with. In fact, when Dickinson added a room to the converted firehouse, he duplicated the character of the old walls with mottled paint on the new ones.

Similarly, in the converted church owned by artists June and George Grammer, old stone basement walls were preserved even though the derelict condition of the entire building demanded refurbishing. What had been a dirt-floored basement is now handsome living quarters in which their stone walls are an integral part of kitchen, living area, and bath. Aside from the modern conveniences, their stone-enclosed dwelling is not very far removed from the caves where walls were first claimed for display by prehistoric man.

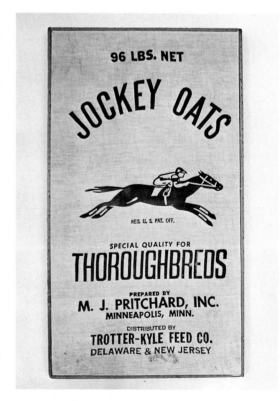

Horse feed bag, *stretched like a painter's canvas, is now in the office of an advertising executive. Pieces of wood fencing salvaged from the beach were used as framing.*

Barbwire and Spanish moss *form a wreath around a mythical horse discovered in the attic. Wreaths can also be made from other found materials such as grapevine and rope.*

Crushed bicycle basket, *reminiscent of Calder's playful wire circus sculpture, hangs on a wall of an East Hampton farmhouse. Rather than altering its character, the owners show the basket as it was found on the roadside, flattened by the wheels of passing cars.*

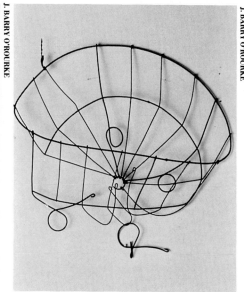

Run-down hat *captured the imagination of artist Bob Levering, who found it in this condition on a city street. After mounting and framing the mangled object, he added it to his assortment of found clothing that hangs like soft sculpture on the walls of his home.*

Stray glove, *gift to Levering from a fellow scavenger, has been caught and frozen mid-gesture in a shadowbox frame. The object is part of an odd assortment of gloves found on city streets and at construction sites.*

Plywood panel, *splashed with color, resembles a minimalist painting. The panel was illuminated with a fluorescent light box and put to work as a decorative object in a large vacant space.*

White sheets *have ascended from beds to drape unsightly walls and ceilings in a temporary dwelling. Fabric remnants can be used similarly as a soft wall covering.*

Ropes, dried weeds, *and other objects hanging in a California studio are periodically replaced. Such simple materials can easily be shifted for a quick change of scenery.*

Bamboo sticks, *collected in the backyard, were nailed in sunburst patterns to pine frames. Glass forms an invisible barrier between indoors and out; the frame lifts out so the window can be opened or cleaned.*

Crafted wall, *above, built from spare pieces of wood by Bill Shields, forms a geometric backboard for the artist's bed. A series of frames superimposed on the raw wood—complete with knots and shadings—display small objects. The wooden Indian at left was built by Shields from scrap metal and bits of wood.*

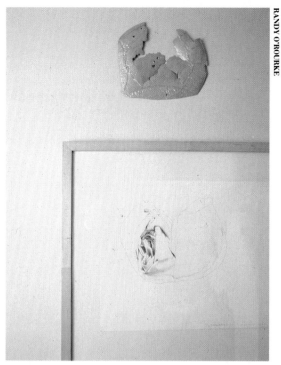

Tin scrap *was crushed and worn when discovered on a New York street. It was glossed over with a coat of silver spray paint and now hangs above a legitimate piece of art.*

Birdseed bag *needed no embellishment to begin a new life as a wall hanging. After the seed was consumed, the bag was tacked above a portable home bar where it appears to be a three-dimensional poster.*

Grass mats *were recycled into window shades for a room that resembles a sophisticated grass hut. Using additional lengths of grass matting, the owner bordered windows with tropical "curtains" tied back with wide pieces of straw. Mullions are composed of bamboo poles fit into the window frame and joined together with leather shoelaces. When the grass shades are lowered, walls become totally covered in straw.*

Labels peeled from tin cans *and cut from seed packets are vivid graphics on this whitewashed wooden wall. Framed in plastic boxes, the labels can easily be changed whenever there is a new supply.*

Styrofoam panels, *formerly used to ship a household appliance, proved to be ideal insulation for a drafty corner window of this mountaintop home in Colorado. The improvised screen turned out to be a good backdrop for the Calder stabile, so it remained a permanent fixture even after the snow melted.*

Photography paper, *referred to as no-seam, creates columns of color in an all-white photography studio. These found objects are actually work materials that take advantage of a blank wall and, in turn, provide decoration.*

Styrofoam packing material, *similar to intaglio, was resurrected as a wall decoration. Well preserved during its previous use, the Styrofoam has been assembled into a geometric bas-relief.*

Magazine clippings, postcards, photos of friends *are an everchanging montage. Rather than being hidden in a drawer or scrapbook, these personal papers are used for display.*

63

64

Four fishing poles *were placed on hold against a wall of a vacation home. Now arranged in an attractive motif, these poles have a separate life as sporting equipment. When the fish are jumping, the owners can grab their gear and go. Skis can be put to similar ornamental use.*

Firewood *creates a changing motif. A recessed compartment holds the wood stacked in random pieces, none of which protrudes into this living room. As the wood is used and replenished, new patterns form.*

Clothing *provides for an ever-changing bed-room wall decoration. In this case, found objects are socks, ties, or sweaters—articles that are usually hidden in drawers or closets—stored on sliding panels.*

Straw bases of Chianti bottles *fill a wall of cubbyholes in a Colorado restaurant. The triangular niches are equally useful for storing wine bottles or colorful napkins.*

Forks from thrift shop *have been attached at the tips to create a wall sconce. The utensils are an ornament for the kitchen.*

Antique automotive radiator part, *surrounded by art objects, resembles a mirror with Art Nouveau details. It catches the light and adds an appealing shape to the room.*

Snapshot *collage makes use of photos that had accumulated in boxes and drawers. Each collage is a sequence of flashbacks, fragments of significant moments that were assembled as a gift to Barbara Ruggiero.*

Discarded stencils, *affixed to canvas by Michael Krieger, hang on a library wall in the artist's home. Sprayed with silver, the stencils appear to have been transformed from plastic to precious metal.*

Polaroid-film case frames—*metal forms from instant film packages—are studded with candid photographs taken by photographer Larry Dale Gordon. No glass cover is needed on these hangings. This disposable decoration is best suited for snapshots, which slide into the frames.*

70

Kitchen tools, *antique and new, suspended on wall are ready for use in a San Francisco home. This functional and decorative arrangement is in the kitchen of an old row house the owners have restored.*

Roots, leaves, and dried flowers, *affixed to a board, create a mural of living things. What appears to be a window view is in actuality an interior wallscape, arranged with rocks and gravel for authenticity.*

edica

rth Atheneum
ford

24 March – 2 May, 1971

Admission free

CHAPTER FIVE
STORAGE

Parkinson's law is applicable to possessions. They expand to fill up the space allotted them. The resulting clutter has the power to transform order into visual chaos unless some provisions are made for storage. This can be accomplished by consulting an architect or cabinetmaker, which will more than likely involve a major investment. *Inventing* storage space is another matter. That simply requires imagination spurred by necessity.

Many found objects have natural nooks and crannies in which to stash possessions. Their shapes suggest practical uses, if not specific ones. Often, if given the chance, found objects can conquer space in addition to decorating it. If a room suffers from storage deficiency, think about improvising with objects that have inherent ability to

Wooden sled, *reminiscent of a hanging butcher rack, holds pots and pans in a kitchen short on storage. With urban space at a premium, room was borrowed from the expansive ceiling. The sled, suspended from hooks and chain link supports, places equipment within reach of the cook. A wooden ladder might similarly be used.*

keep things in place. Unlike built-in compartments, invented storage units are mobile, useful in more rooms than one and, above all, imaginative. Though rooms vary in function and size, they all have predictable surfaces that can hold belongings—that is, they have floors, walls, and ceilings.

Containers of various sizes and shapes can be positioned on the floor near chairs and sofas to serve as catchalls. Boxes, such as old wooden crates—some of which have original stenciling as part of their charm—are more than adequate receptacles for magazines, toys, and firewood. The corrugated circular forms that hold wine bottles inside cartons have potential use as rustic holders for rolled newspapers and magazines.

Rather than let magazines fall where they may, take advantage of other commonplace objects that can serve as organizers. Bicycle baskets and bushel baskets commonly found at fruit stands and markets are handy storage units, small enough to tuck under a chair

or to mount on the wall.

The wall is another dependable surface to lean on (or hang on). Of all the natural objects found outdoors, twigs take to the walls quite readily. Bound together in crisscross fashion with twine, they can be mounted on the wall as an instant towel rack. Rows of twigs, nailed together in grid formation, serve as a natural-looking wall unit for hanging lightweight kitchen utensils. Nature provides hooks also in the form of tree limbs with stumps where branches have broken off. Hung on a bathroom wall, the limb would welcome hand towels or bathrobes. Picturesque shopping bags can be used as wall-hung compartments for laundry, rolls of wrapping paper, or colored tissue. Simply attach the handles to one small nail or a pegboard hook. The bag should be sturdy enough to manage a light load, but should it begin to give way, replace it with another.

Shelves and storage systems are ideally placed along blank walls. To create ample shelf units, position one pair of black or orange driveway sealer cans (their labels removed) on either end of a six-foot weathered board. Repeat the arrangement on a second level so that the cans are lined up in columns, the boards positioned as shelf units. It is advisable to fill the cans with rocks so that they can support weight on the shelves.

The ceiling provides an inviting expanse for hanging objects. So long as it is low enough that the suspended objects remain within reach, the ceiling can be a supplemental storage area. Caterer Martha Stewart hangs masses of baskets from hooks that dot her kitchen rafters. The varied shapes are visible from below and readily accessible during cooking marathons. If your ceiling is unusually high, there are any number of objects that could be suspended, thereby making the ceiling seem lower. One chef attached a wooden ladder parallel to his hard-to-reach ceiling. Fastened directly to the ceiling by way of large screw eyes, the ladder's rungs are convenient places to hang pots and utensils from S-shaped hooks. The object is also an architectural element above the work area. A rusted garden rake, inverted and fastened to the ceiling, is another possibility; utensils would hang from its metal teeth. A branch could also be suspended from the ceiling via hooks and hanging chains fastened to each end. Hung horizontally, these swinglike objects—similar to hanging butcher racks—will hold pots

and kitchen utensils suspended from **S**-shaped hooks. A simple wooden hanger can be hung the same way or a portion of beach fence with its slats serving as hangers for kitchen tools. As with any hanging object, there should be plenty of headroom so you are not knocked unconscious by a dangling pot.

The purpose of extra storage space is to subtract clutter, not increase it. Found objects, therefore, must have a strategic place—either against a wall, in an out-of-the-way place on the floor, or overhead. After you have determined what possessions need organizing and what space you are willing to sacrifice for open storage, set out to find an imaginative solution.

Log with ample cranny *has been put to use to hold a parade of wooden utensils lined up for action. The log's niche might also support an open cookbook or serve as a rack for several books.*

Biscuit tins *on a lacquered table in an elegant apartment in a New York City skyscraper. The tins are at peace in such surroundings, their color in harmony with the blue armchairs.*

Wire bin, *which formerly served as a vegetable stand, has the sleek lines of a contemporary storage unit. The collapsible mesh rack is used for stacking magazines and records; the lower section holds bulkier items.*

J. BARRY O'ROURKE

Clam basket *serves two purposes in a farmhouse. When not being used at the nearby beach, the seasoned wire basket is an extra receptacle for magazines stationed next to an easy chair.*

Packing mold, *typical of those used for shipping appliances, simulates a shelf with built-in bookends and serves as a bedside caddy on this quilt-covered table. The Styrofoam tray could also house sewing materials or cosmetics and a variety of personal effects.*

Galvanized-wire fence—*heavier gauge than chicken wire*—*is the material used to structure these ingenious storage systems. Designer David Murray discovered new applications for the fencing when a friend asked if he could improve the quality of her kennel cages. While experimenting with discarded wire, Murray developed a sturdy frame by welding together steel strips with wire grids and wrapping the frames with rope. He proceeded to make these variations based on the same principle: a horizontal storage unit for books, stereo, and TV; an arched shelf unit, hung from a window frame, wrapped in yellow plastic rope; a shelf unit for large platters, with rope dividers stretched from one level to another. This sort of galvanized wire, welded into gridwork, could also be attached to a wall as hanging storage for a collection of tools.*

Graphic cookie tins *are clustered on a lunch table with other objects of the owner's affection.*

Soap boxes are decorative organizers for pins, buttons, and all manner of odds and ends on a bedside table. Commercial packaging such as this is an alternative to cloisonné and lacquer boxes.

Imported ricotta cans and cheese crocks *are handy catchalls in a kitchen. Once the contents have been devoured, the tins gain visibility as utensil organizers. Rather than take up drawer space, the tools stand in one convenient spot within arm's reach.*

Cardboard box, *from a shipment of Cutty Sark, is a no-nonsense container that has apparent potential as a colorful accent. Here it is incorporated with earthenware objects on a mantel of brick.*

CHRIS MEAD

86

Care package in a crate *at a country house. Using vegetable crates that he collects for such occasions, the owner organizes books and refreshments to offer weekend guests. Sturdier than a tray, the crate can be transported from one lounging place to the next.*

Old crate, *found in an apple orchard, bears its original owner's name. Presently a chair-side holder for magazines, it could also store an ample collection of toys in a family room. Cutout handles make it portable as well as versatile. Emptied of odds and ends, turned upside down and fitted with a tray, it could pass as an antique end table. A collection of boxes such as this, turned on their sides and stacked against a wall, could function as rugged-looking storage units.*

Soda crates, *constructed of sturdy wood, were nailed to the wall of a Colorado shop where they display a vast collection of mugs. Arranged in a similar unit, the rectangular bins could be used to hold toys, books, bar glasses and bottles, or sporting equipment.*

CHRIS MEAD

Terra-cotta flue pipe, *found gathering dust in the basement, appeared to have promise as an umbrella stand. Moved to the front hallway, it now collects umbrellas and equipment that would ordinarily demand closet space.*

Fruit crate, *which once was used for shipping mangoes, has been adapted for armchair use— as a hanging rack for periodicals in a family room. Secured with two bands of the same fabric that covers the chair, the rack is within easy reach of the reader. Original labels were left intact.*

Wood frame surrounded by metal stripping *(possibly a part from a ship's deck)* with *the addition of distressed wood shelves became a spice rack. Mounted on a swivel in a San Francisco kitchen, its contents visible from two sides, the frame has evolved considerably since it was found in a vacant lot.*

Cupboard of salvaged wood *was constructed as a storage unit for food-processor parts in the same kitchen. The pieces of wood, collected from construction sites, are arranged so that their patterns interplay.*

CHAPTER SIX

FOR PLANTS AND FLOWERS

Nature is an inexhaustible source of design ideas. No wonder the trend toward decorating with plants and flowers has gained such popularity. Robust-looking plants and freshly cut flowers bring such life and color to our rooms that communing with nature indoors has become a favorite pastime.

Elvin McDonald, author of *The World Book of House Plants* and a noted authority on gardening, lives in a New York City apartment that is a blossoming interior landscape of some three hundred plants thriving year round. They grow in sundry found containers that he collects "for the personality they give to a room." Indeed, each plant takes on a character of its own, according to the manner in which it is planted.

Among Elvin McDonald's most spectacular containers are discarded wooden cheese flats from nearby markets, which provide ideal containers for bulbs and small plants. He lines them with plastic, covering the whole interior to make the flats "absolutely waterproof." The bulbs or plants are positioned in the containers and surrounded by pure sphagnum peat moss. Deeper cheese flats house small potted plants such as begonia and English ivy, covered to the rim with moss or other attractive mulch.

Many potential plant containers of this genre regularly make it home from market to kitchen. Baskets used to hold mushrooms and berries make fine planting pots once they are waterproofed with a layer of heavy-duty foil or plastic sheeting (stapled to the rim). In early spring, if you buy flats of dwarf zinnias, petunias, and pansies, place several plants in these wooden baskets and watch them grow into decorative bouquets. The basket is an interim step before transplanting flowers into the garden. Egg cartons of white plastic may seem useless once the eggs are emptied, but the cartons can serve as containers for seedlings. Fill each compartment with a planting medium, such as pasteurized potting soil; plant the seeds, moisten, and set the egg carton in a bright window. The seedlings planted in this manner provide one another with humidity and will grow at a rapid clip.

Also from the kitchen, commercial stoneware crocks, emptied of their mustard or jam, resemble handcrafted ceramics and make long-lasting planters in which to root plant clippings. Bottles that have strayed from the kitchen or grocery to the beach are often worth carting home, particularly if they have been weathered and improved upon by nature. Use them as vases for cut flowers. Empty perfume and cordial bottles also make beautiful vases. A few cut flowers will need little arranging; let them form their own graceful patterns in these small glass containers.

Biscuit tins, complete with their graphically designed labels, have aesthetic value as colorful plant

Recycled hubcap *is now a modernistic stand for flowers. A florist's pin holder, placed in the center of the hubcap, secures one long amaryllis blossom. Waterproof floral clay surrounds the center where two more amaryllis blossoms are fastened to the pins. Circles of silver foil are scattered around the disk; silver lamé covers the table.*

containers. They are bound to rust if filled with water, so it is best to line them with foil before placing a moist plant inside. Coffee tins can also serve as decorative containers—for coffee plants among other things. Unroasted beans will grow inside the cans if you cover a few beans with potting soil and place the can in a sunny window.

Natural objects can be made to serve as containers too. Gray weathered woods, deep green moss, clay-colored rocks, and fresh vegetables—all earthy tones of nature—are compatible with virtually every live (or dried) plant and floral arrangement. The transition from natural material to container may involve little more than bringing the object indoors. Certain found objects, however, require some special handiwork.

Twigs, gathered from the yard, can be used to frame the base of a potted plant. Circle the pot with a group of matched twigs, holding them in place with two rows of twine, one tied near the top, the other around the base. The effect is that of a handmade basket. Rocks and pebbles can also be shaped into containers or supports for greenery and blossoms. Designers Bob Patino and Vincente Wolf use rocks as holders for their cut flowers. Piled around the stems in a shallow saucer, the rocks appear to produce their own blooms.

Vegetables and fruit can be reborn as containers. An acorn squash, with its fluted bottle green skin and orange markings, lends itself to transformation into a bud vase. With some dexterity, the squash can easily become a container for an autumn bouquet. Using a paring knife, simply carve out a big enough hole for a tubular glass florist's vial to fit the length of the squash. Insert long-stemmed flowers, such as anemone, daisy, or rose, and fill the glass vial with water. The vases can be displayed individually or clustered in a group. The squash will probably stay garden fresh several days before it must be discarded.

A scooped-out watermelon half can also be put to decorative use. Once you have removed the fruit, stick the stems of zinnias, marigolds, and daisies into the cavity; the flowers will feed on the natural juices remaining in the skin. This should be made the same day of your party, since it is a one-occasion container. Save the flowers for another planter.

Armed with a few basic design principles, you can experiment with a variety of natural and man-made containers. One rule of thumb: the less colorful the container, the more colorful the flowers. Conversely, boldly colored containers are more limiting. Allow the plant or flower to dictate the shape of its holder. Think of balancing the two: a bushy lilac requires a sturdy base, while a slender daffodil will stand tall in a bed of rocks. By and large, tall growing flowers seem at home in tall vases and short-stemmed plants look quite natural in shallow baskets.

The eye is the best judge of good proportion, but if you would like an expert's opinion, here is what McDonald recommends: the height and width of a container should be ⅓ or ½ that of the plant. It is safe to assume that a 6-inch container will suit an 18-inch-tall plant. Top-heavy plants need to be transferred to a larger pot in order to achieve balance.

J. BARRY O'ROURKE

Common black plastic litter bag, *which manages to look like the same material as the black lampshade, houses several potted plants on top of a traditional console. The bag protects wood surfaces and surrounds the arrangement in a shiny pouch.*

Flowers in a flat crate *seem as natural as if they were growing outdoors. The crate has been waterproofed with foil and layered with moist florist foam. Dutch iris, tulips, and daffodils are arranged under a carpet of live moss. The wire wastepaper basket holds a plant surrounded by moss.*

Rope-bound logs *form an elevated stand for a plant-filled bowl. As in a woodland setting, the greenery spills over fallen logs. In this case, the logs have been uniformly cut and tightly bound to create a firm plant stand. The combination of rugged bark and the lacquered tabletop is oriental in its grace and simplicity.*

Colorado logs, tied with packing twine, *stand upright to form a circular holder for dried flowers and pine branches. A transparent plastic bowl, placed in the center of the circle of logs, contains the flowers and greenery. Pine branches are also tucked in between the logs. Tufts of Spanish moss, one surrounding the base of the logs, the other a "nest" for walnuts, are placed near a bunch of cinnamon sticks.*

Ball of moss, tied with twine, *appears to have given birth to a beautiful orchid. The moss encases the plastic container and provides a natural surrounding for the delicate flower.*

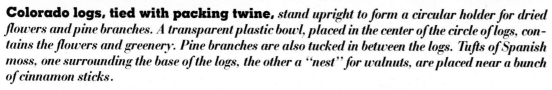

Pebbles found at the beach *are creative camouflage for glass containers holding reedlike agapanthus. The mound of pebbles has been arranged on a mantel, creating the illusion that the flowers are growing out of a rocky oasis. A similar effect may be achieved with shells and chunks of beach glass piled around glass vials holding miniature flowers.*

Smooth weather-worn logs *correspond to the aged wood of this Bavarian trunk. One L-shaped log supports another lying on its side, and a third is positioned in front. A potted begonia sits in the background; a cluster of grapes is cradled in the curve of the log.*

Discarded crate, which has been waterproofed with an interior lining of plastic and a rug remnant tacked to the underside, holds an indoor garden in a city home. A bed of gravel provides drainage for the clay-potted plants. The crate also functions as a space divider in a wide-open loft.

Humble plastic pot, a staple of nurseries and garden-supply stores, was considered fine enough to be invited indoors. The plain black container is used as a substitute for glazed ceramic.

Garbage-can lid serves as a giant saucer. The handle has been hammered flat so the sturdy tin disk rests evenly on top of an old trunk turned coffee table. The Ruggiero children filled the lid with gravel to make a rocky bed for a trio of bonsai plants, each in a different ceramic pot. Flowering plants can be arranged in a similar manner to form a colorful mobile garden. At Christmas, the shiny tin lid becomes a festive tray laden with miniature poinsettias and cactus. To herald spring, tulips, daffodils, and narcissus plants are set among the rocks.

Cardboard box, *complete with its shipping labels, was left in its original state after the top was removed. The box is an unpretentious container for a cluster of dried flowers on a bleached pine table. Florist foam holds the flowers in place.*

Styrofoam shipping form *from a stereo has a long-playing record as a plant container. Looking every bit as distinguished as contemporary ceramics, the form neatly accommodates two potted plants.*

J. BARRY O'ROURKE

Water-soaked bed of crushed glass *in a shell-shaped ceramic dish contains an exotic plant. A wire holder supports the flowering plant. A beach shell could be used as an alternative and filled with smooth pieces of beach glass. Covered with a thin layer of water, the glass glistens as if washed by the waves.*

J. BARRY O'ROURKE

J. BARRY O'ROURKE

Brightly colored paper bags *in soft sculptural forms are used as containers for centerpieces. Cans of water have been placed inside to hold the bouquets. Cardboard tubes were stood on end and taped together with heavy-duty packing tape that has been camouflaged by paper streamers. A stand, fashioned from a cardboard box, supports the paper fiesta.*

Dust mop *has been "planted" to camouflage an unsightly container. The orchid rises above what appears to be a cluster of tropical roots.*

Miniature cordial bottles *make delicate bud vases. This tabletop is transformed into a tiny garden; blossoms snipped from house plants change with the seasons.*

Silver champagne box *was spared on its way to the trash can because of its decorative quality and ideal proportions for holding tall flowers. The flowers rest in the champagne bottle, refilled with plain water, which sits inside the box. The bouquet of pastel flowers imitates the floral design on the overstuffed chair, as well as that on the slender container.*

Empty yogurt container *becomes a perfect resting place for a large petaled flower. Take a boldly colored red-toned blossom, such as the amaryllis pictured here, and cut all but two inches away from the stem. Weight the cup with a bed of pebbles and add some water The blossom should unfold just above the rim, an effusion of nature overflowing from the cup. A variety of containers in different colors might be used, matched with flowers of similar or contrasting hues.*

DANNON
Plain
LOWFAT
YOGURT
NET WT. 8 OZ. (227g)

Discarded meat chopper, *one of the found objects displayed at Longwood Gardens, the Du Pont family estate in Pennsylvania, resembles a piece of primitive sculpture perched on the top rung of a handcrafted ladder. A single pot of African violets, fit snugly inside the feeder, gives the relic new aesthetic value. The same ladder is used by the Longwood staff of gardeners to display house plants on graduated levels, an idea that visitors can duplicate with a stepstool or library ladder. The conservatory, open to the public throughout the year, was funded by the Du Pont family.*

Tins and bottles *mix with paintings, porcelains, and fine antique furnishings in plant columnist C. Z. Guest's New York apartment. These mass-produced containers for wafers, ginger ale, olive oil, and instant coffee possess strong design qualities that enable them to hold their own in such elegant surroundings. Mrs. Guest collects commercial tins and bottles for their appealing shapes and colors and uses them to display flowers from the greenhouse of her property on Long Island. When visitors admire her floral arrangements, she often presents them as parting gifts.*

AMERICAN FASHION

Plastic oil can and gas-additive container, *stripped of their labels, resemble the smooth china of a nearby lamp. Sleek as the distant cityscape, these pure white vases mix easily with traditional furnishings.*

108

Shampoo bottle *has been washed, rinsed, and shorn of its label. The plastic container is a simple form that can hold a small bouquet or a single flower.*

109

Giant logs, rusted cans, bushel baskets, and crates, *diverse in texture and size, serve as containers and platforms for flowering plants in the brick-paved Ruggiero loggia. Weathered oil cans in graduated heights show off vibrant cineraria; hollowed-out logs, found in a vacant lot, are a perfect fit for pots of primrose; an old barbecue suspended from a wall holds chrysanthemums and ivy.*

Roll of industrial packing tape *has been enlisted as a stand for a flowering plant rooted in a ball of moss. The unusual arrangement rests on a table made of thread spools.*

Tops of cheese boxes *used to support plants. Filled with a bed of pebbles, one lid holds a flowering plant, the other a monochromatic grouping of artichokes and apples. The gaily colored box top, turned on its side, is purely decorative.*

Wooden crates, *found at neighborhood grocery stores, are ideally suited for forcing spring bulbs in a bright window. Similar crates can also be used as natural-looking containers for a variety of houseplants.*

Tissue box *with a botanical design contains an arrangement of delphiniums in a glass jam jar filled with water. Small square tissue boxes in colorful patterns can be used to house a single potted plant or cut flowers such as these.*

Chestnut-puree can, *with glaze-finished label, doubles as a Christmas decoration on a festively dressed table. It holds evergreens and white silk edelweiss, neither of which requires water for survival. Resembling a cachepot of fine Limoges, the can is clearly at home with silver and candlelight.*

Bags of amaryllis *bloom in the shadow of a banana tree. Plain brown paper bags dress up the containers of blossoming plants, such as these two flowering amaryllis stationed on a marble-topped bureau. The bags can be pinched closed so that they hug the stem of the flower and enclose the pot in soft folds (no need to tie with a string).*

Mushroom baskets and paper bags *are readily available containers for potted plants. Each basket is filled with two different potted plants and grouped together in an entryway. A slatted wood crate (found at the vegetable market) acts as a stand for a pot planted with a single amaryllis blossom and covered with a paper bag.*

Wire light guard, *used by workmen, was discovered in a basement. Reminiscent of filigree, the wire frame holds a glass of tulips and hyacinth on a window ledge in a country home. Old wire baskets, fitted with glass containers, would work as well.*

Vintage milk-bottle carrier *was converted to a flower basket. Slender glass containers accommodate long-stemmed and short-stemmed flowers, bunched in individual bouquets that appear to be one profuse arrangement.*

117

CHAPTER SEVEN

SMALL POSSESSIONS

Out of necessity we shop for accent pieces that fulfill a specific need, perform a definite function, or simply fill a void. We search the marketplace for frames to display photographs and artwork, lamps for reading and for highlighting areas of our rooms, and ornaments for sheer pleasure. What we don't necessarily consider are everyday objects with more versatility than we give them credit for. Among the miscellanea that multiplies over the years may be objects you will find more desirable than anything money can buy.

Designer Mario Buatta prefers to call accent pieces possessions. "It makes them sound much more personal. Rooms are not like cars; there's no such thing as an optional accessory. Everything must either have a personal association, bring back a memory, or express an interest."

Dock bumper guard, which had been washed up on the Pacific shore, poses as a fine antique perch for a Renaissance cherub. The lowly object bears a weathered patina nearly identical to that of the art it supports; the angel has been equipped with a smart new parasol.

How does one go about ornamenting a home? First, think of what possessions mean the most to you and then find an appropriate place to display them. If you have a collection of prized things, found or otherwise acquired, be bold—group them on a table where they can be observed in passing and at close range. This grouping of diverse objects is what English designer David Hicks refers to as tablescapes. "Objects arranged as landscapes on a horizontal surface become an art form," he explains. "What is important is not how valuable or inexpensive your objects are, but the care and feeling with which you arrange them."

Equally important are the memories they evoke. Sentimental tokens, reminders of childhood days, souvenirs from places you have traveled, they all reveal more than words can say.

As a boy, Franklin Delano Roosevelt collected so many souvenirs from his nature studies and sailing trips that his desk top was laden with memorabilia. His presidential desk, on display in Hyde Park, New York, is heaped with more personal objects than it seems able to hold, its writing surface obliterated by possessions. For many adults, the childlike instinct to scavenge increases with age, and there is no reason why the most humble objects we find cannot reside with possessions of considerable monetary value.

For those whose taste runs to Royal Crown Derby, Limoges, Noguchi, or van Gogh, found objects may seem out of their element when speaking of decorative accents. However, these humble objects created by man and nature can take their places on shelves and tables next to the finest works of art and craftsmanship. All it takes is a little imagination—and a leap of faith.

Found objects can be called upon to fill in for mass-produced accents if we give them a chance. When artist Alexander Calder transformed a flattened olive oil tin into a tray, he made a lowly object purposeful; the tin assumed a new

119

identity. In reexamining the simplest objects, we can often come up with new ideas for their use. Think of a wooden crate as a platform for sculpture, a tin can as a light fixture, a chunk of cement as a bookend. Then put it to work in its new role. As a way of stimulating ideas for found objects as accents, collect what appeals to you for shape, color, texture, and uniqueness. Put them away and when the time comes that you feel the urge to shop, you can do so at home. You will begin to see what objects may be able to frame snapshots, support books, display art, or light a corner—and what can be used for pure ornament.

Finally, consider this Japanese custom when arranging your found objects as accessories. To herald each new season, Japanese families change all the pictures, wall hangings, and other accessories in their rooms, replacing them with ones that are more in harmony with a particular season. Rearranging possessions is a way of refreshing the mind and spirit, a reawakening of memories. Whether you choose to focus on one special object or myriad possessions, there is great pleasure to be derived in the quiet contemplation of them as they change with the seasons.

Mixing paddle *from industrial food mixer, retrieved from a city street, poses as tabletop sculpture. Its classic shape is compatible with a variety of more traditional decorative objects.*

Steam iron, *relieved from active duty, now works as a bookend. The iron's silvery body matches the textured tin walls and makes an impressive case for repositioning rather than discarding household appliances that no longer work.*

Styrofoam packing material, *which once protected a toy, was hand painted by a resourceful child and transformed into a frame. A family photograph was pasted in the center.*

Styrofoam wig stand *was removed from the garbage and recast as sculpture. Standing on a marble-topped table, the synthetic form looks as if it too might have been created from stone—an obvious piece of trompe l'oeil at second glance.*

Wax dripping *from a candle was carefully removed and brought home as a reminder of an enjoyable dinner party. Among the many images the slender particle evokes is an ice sculpture in the process of melting.*

Frame for candy hearts, *from a Valentine gift box, holds a uniform group of family close-ups. The top of a wine crate, embellished with a château, is a backdrop for a group of miniature houses on this wall unit, built with twigs. Next to the townscape, a wreath of dried flowers.*

123

Stones from the Long Island coast, *placed on a stone gray platform, create a serene oriental vignette. An earth-colored lacquer tray holds rocks that relate in shape to the lamp and in color to the entire room.*

Stones *arranged in a bowl as if they were an assortment of fruit. The rounded, monochromatic forms, souvenirs of beachcombing, echo the shapes and colors of furnishings in a converted firehouse. The stone-colored wall has been left in its original state.*

124

Stones and fragments of bones, *collected for their sculptural lines, are placed on a cloth-draped table as ornaments. The head is a plaster casting of the collector's.*

Coconut, *found on a Florida beach, has been covered with gold paint and assimilated by more serious art objects. When it comes to mixing fine art with found objects, the main requisite is a sense of humor.*

Piece of horn, *with a shell resting in its curve, has been fashioned into a graceful wall light. A tiny votive candle glows from its hiding place inside the translucent shell, casting light on the natural forms.*

126

Rock in shape of Nantucket *is the memento of a family vacation. The Ruggiero children were challenged to find a native rock form duplicating the island's silhouette. Embellished with a hand-drawn map of Nantucket, the rock has assumed a permanent place on this library shelf.*

Geological forms, hardened layers of sand, *sit atop a weatherbeaten table covered with a layer of broken beach glass. The primitive-looking wood form that stands on a block of beach wood was found among weeds and vines in a vacant lot. The circular shapes appear to mimic the round window cut out of the background wall.*

Beach glass *can be used as a covering for shelves, tables, and potted plants. The colorful translucent fragments are decorative elements that require no formal arrangement.*

Fireplug head, *fashioned into a sculptural light socket, was found in a basement. Put to better use as a temporary fixture, it has become a source of amusement as well as illumination.*

Tree-trunk lamp *appears to have grown where it stands, surrounded by wood and earth-color materials. With electrical wiring and the addition of an inverted basket, an actual lamp was devised from this organic form.*

Discarded lamp base *has a new purpose in life, stationed on a country-style chest. With its frosted light bulb from the local hardware store, the tall fixture is reminiscent of an old-fashioned streetlight.*

Jug wine bottles *perform as bedroom lamps in the guest room of a country house. The perfectly matched pair, as naïve as folk art, have been electrically wired and fitted with unobtrusive white shades.*

Broken pieces of pottery, *embedded in plaster, form a lamp base in a country home. The fragments are arranged as a colorful mosaic.*

Center of wagon wheel *was made into a hanging light fixture. Suspended from a chain, it now hangs in a hallway. A single bulb sends light through its apertures.*

Brown paper bag *has gone from supermarket to sublime. Mounted on a wire frame, it now serves as a lampshade. In the background, a framed photograph by Richard Avedon of a workman's glove found in the street.*

Parasol *camouflages a light fixture in a Key West home. Wire was used to fasten umbrella to fixture, with ample room left between the parchment shade and light bulb to eliminate fire hazards.*

Olive-oil can *has been recycled into a decorative lamp base. The can adds lively pattern and color to a traditionally designed room.*

Plastic hose *from a clothes dryer is now a sculptural object. Fitted with a string of tiny Christmas bulbs, the knotted hose snakes across the mantel casting light en route.*

129

Wire plant baskets, *covered with muslin, are transformed into soft wall sconces. The muslin was dipped in plaster and wrapped around the wire frames. The shell-like forms diffuse and direct light upward, causing soft halos to appear on the ceiling.*

Shells, stones, and beach glass *are displayed in tiny compartments of a leaf-shaped Japanese paint box and on top of a stack of tiny dishes. The compact container that holds small treasures is a microcosm of the marine world in the front yard of a house along the California coast.*

Whalebone stands with a cement relic *on a bedside table. The fan-shaped bone presents a solid mass behind the straw flower container; the deeply creviced chunk of cement, also a found object, could be mistaken for a fragment of pre-Columbian art. Although one material is natural and the other man-made, they are similar in texture.*

Old buzz saw *retains its cutting edge as sculpture. Traced with rust and signs of use, the blade looks right at home among the earth-tone furniture and organic materials in the room.*

Bits of wood, *weathered by storms and tides, were collected at the New Jersey shore. Nailed together in an orderly formation, they were framed with pieces of beach fence. Painted pieces of wood, interspersed among natural fragments, stand out like tattered book jackets on a library shelf.*

Top of wine crate *makes an excellent cutting board, the perfect size for a portable bar. Available in a range of designs from simple French châteaus to intricate winery crests, the boards would be an inspired gift for the connoisseur— and might serve as proof that only the best wines are provided.*

Hay from a New England barn *was stuffed into a wooden bowl and trimmed to imitate a bird's nest, complete with a pretend chick perched on top. Small twigs may be used to achieve a similar whimsical nest.*

Bundle of twigs *sits atop a mantel in the living room of a California house. This utilitarian arrangement, used to start fires, lends a spark of interest before it goes up in smoke.*

Flower blossoms, *collected from wilted bouquets, can be left in open dishes as fragrant decoration or wrapped in fabric as sachets for closets and drawers. Rather than throw flower arrangements away, place flower heads in a large container where their subtle colors and fragrances mingle.*

Driftwood *elevated to a pedestal stands against a stucco wall. The imposing form is framed by the angular space.*

Sea anemones and dried fruit *are exotic forms in a bowl of potpourri. A similar mixture might be composed of crushed flower petals with whole dried lemons and pomegranates.*

Old phonograph *waiting for the local garbage collector has been cranked up as art. To its finder's surprise, the aged machine actually worked.*

Twigs in a basket *have been domesticated from the Colorado landscape. Such ordinary found objects become unusual when they are employed in new ways.*

Wooden slats and bamboo poles *create a visual boundary for a selection of found objects in the corner of a bedroom. A lampshade fashioned from a basket and bird feathers, a chunk of beach wood, and a mirror framed in shells are among the man-made and natural treasures.*

138

Dried root *was found in Mexico. Coveted for its resemblance to a footed bowl, the root was filled with dried gourds and planted on a shelf.*

Cat-food cans *are silvery holders for votive candles. The perfect depth to protect candles from winds and crossdrafts, the cans have been carefully arranged to throw off rows of soft light.*

Mass-produced bottles *such as this, which once held grape juice, are likely holders for candles. Popular light fixtures in college dorms and country pubs, the candle-in-a-bottle is one of the more familiar uses of found objects.*

140

Plastic containers from a delicatessen *are holders for votive candles on a desk top. The hourglass shapes masquerade as contemporary crystal among a collection of oriental decorative objects.*

Flattened beer can *has been recycled to perform a new function. It serves as a tray for a fat candle whose drippings simply add more character to the all-American object.*

141

Cigarette packages *are arranged in a kaleidoscopic pattern in a London flat. The Players cigarette casings can assume a variety of decorative shapes, depending on sleight of hand.*

Wooden clothespins *were assembled into a sculptural cross. The old-fashioned pins, elementary as building blocks, hold together securely so that tall forms are easily mastered.*

Used matchsticks *are the building materials for a wood-framed cross, its texture reminiscent of handwoven straw.*

142

Bamboo poles *about to be carted away from a local tackle shop were reeled in for ornament. The window moldings have been painted in mottled tones to complement the coloring of bamboo. Arranged in a tall pot embellished with moose antlers, the poles reach up toward the ceiling, functioning as an architectural element in the room.*

Discarded lawnmower part *once lay on the front lawn of a house in East Hampton, New York. Mounted on wood, its humble origins now well in the past, this found object looks like a close relation of African art.*

Wimple sticks *were found in an abandoned tack room, then cut off at the top. The curious pair—a challenge to the imagination—stands on a shelf in a crisp white kitchen.*

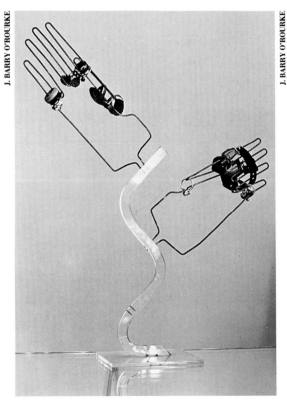

Glove rack, *tossed in the trash by a display company, found a more receptive home. A handy form that organizes everyday jewels, favorite gems, and imitations, the object performs as contemporary sculpture as well.*

Metal and wood scraps, *selected by artist Bob Levering, contribute to his sculptural compositions referred to as "street art." This arrangement of weathered bits and parts appears in a kettle that has also seen better days.*

Glass tube, filled with fish-tank gravel, *chopsticks, and plastic jewelry, is what interior designer Arthur Ferber refers to as a "space flower arrangement." In this minimal environment, accessories pose as architectural elements, purposely spare so as not to intrude.*

Plastic display rack, *which once held travel brochures, was picked up from a city street. It stands like a fanciful pagoda in a corner of a living room, its translucent surfaces shimmering with light.*

Barnacled wood, *from a Long Island boatyard, has been docked on a table in Connecticut. The marine artifact—precisely as it was found—mingles with more aristocratic possessions such as Egyptian patchwork and cloisonné on a fine lacquer chest.*

Whalebone *found in Mexico rests on a cocktail table in a New York City apartment. The candle holders are discarded meat hooks discovered on the street in Manhattan's SoHo section.*

J. BARRY O'ROURKE

RANDY O'ROURKE

J. BARRY O'ROURKE

RANDY O'ROURKE

Fallen leaves *picked up on the Ruggiero property were placed on construction paper, pressed between two pieces of glass, and framed with heavy-duty tape. The montage was a gift from Mariette Uldry, a friend whose autumn visit the leaves recall. The mounted leaves rest behind a collection of rocks, coral, beach glass, and shells.*

Unfinished needlework canvases *were destined for obscurity until their decorative quality was recognized. Displayed in plastic boxes, the weavings illustrate the potential use of textile fragments as colorful accents.*

146

Shells in baskets, *souvenirs of family trips, sit on the floor of a New York City apartment. Treasured but not overprotected, these assortments of shells are frequently used as humble doorstops.*

Bowl of white blossoms *includes dried flowers plucked from many different bouquets. The delicate arrangement—as lovely as bisque sculpture—contains blossoms selected for their similar tones.*

Bed pad, *sewn into a pillow cover, has been strewn with a garden of flowers in acrylic paints. The design, a convincing replica of needlepoint, owes its texture to diagonal quilting.*

Inside of broken clock, *which couldn't be fixed, was left on a table and forgotten. When the black metal gears began to attract attention, this spare part was kept permanently in place to make a timeless statement.*

Film cases *answer the need for picture frames. Ideal sizes for most snapshots, these cases are leftovers from instant film packages. The vents have been folded down to act as stands.*

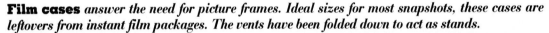

Packing material *that contained two vases was preserved as a decorative object. Its hollowed-out spaces echo the sinuous curves of the two ceramic urns.*

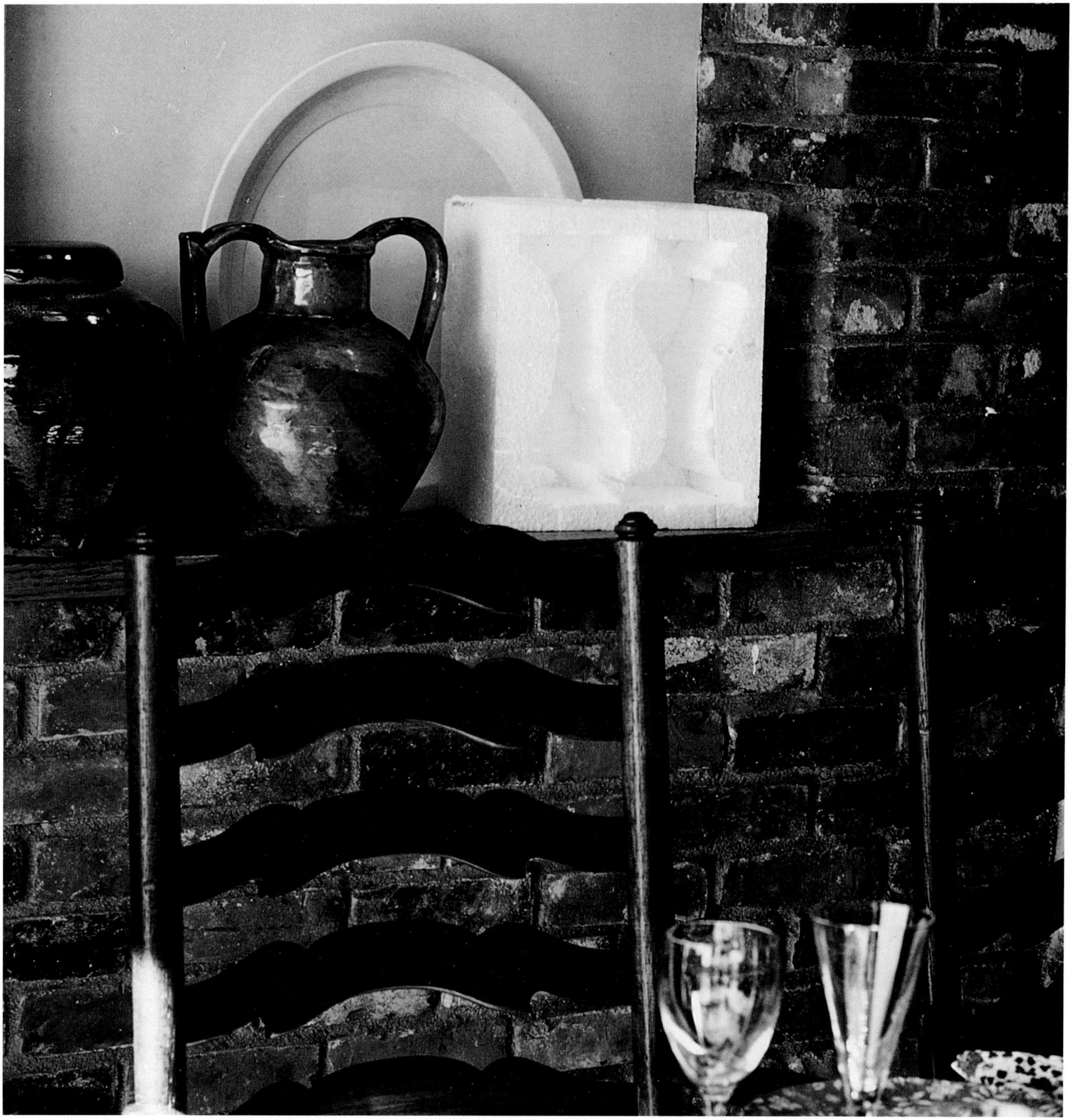

J. BARRY O'ROURKE

CHAPTER EIGHT

IN THE OPEN AIR

There is a world of freedom outside our houses, an endless expanse where nature, not man, is responsible for the way things are. We can, however, impose our ideas on nature, deftly tailoring its spaces to extend our living quarters.

To introduce a personal note among the natural elements has always been a challenge. Primitive man rearranged stones to mark his place on the landscape; the ancient Assyrians cultivated gardens on barren plains, the earliest Japanese created natural tableaux using water, rocks, and trees as an artist would use paints and brushes. The legendary gardens of Japan are confined to small areas where natural objects convey a feeling of serenity and order in a chaotic world: a miniature bridge of sticks over a river of stones; trunks of trees as dividers for flower beds; bamboo poles as barriers between adjoining yards.

Nature's familiar surroundings can be the starting point for feats of invention. Since they are indigenous to the land, natural objects, such as the stones rearranged by primitive man and the primary elements used by the Japanese, are priceless design materials for patios and gardens.

Instead of planting delicate flowers in his windswept yard, San Francisco designer Ron Mann has landscaped it with sculptural forms of rocks and whalebone that will not yield to the climate. His courtyard is a mystical kingdom of found objects. Living in a changeable atmosphere on the California coast where weather patterns shift abruptly from temperate to turbulent, Mann has learned to respect nature's wiles. "We have nature as a powerful force at our fingertips. I recognize the strong features of an environment and use them rather than alter them," he says. His garden changes with the weather—

inorganic forms taking on new beauty, bathed in light or pelted by the rain.

On the crest of his lawn, Mann has arranged rocks in such a manner that they repeat the jagged coastline in the distance. In lieu of formal garden furniture, this rock formation—heaped with cushions—functions as a stationary sofa. The found objects on his property are integral parts of the terrain, meant to live outdoors year round.

Materials derived from nature can be used to tame it. Instead of a formal arrangement of flowering plants, a mosaic of shells and stones in a classical geometric design might be placed in a bed of soil. A cluster of logs in different sizes and heights might be stood on end and surrounded by low-lying flowering plants or ivy, creating a sculptural silhouette and a place for children to play. Crushed shells, stones, and pine needles can be used to surface garden paths.

Nature is also receptive to manmade objects, if they can survive

Beach stones, polished by the surf, sit on a rugged pedestal that marks a trail to the ocean on the seaside property of designers Ron Mann and Ivy Rosequist. Beyond the Brancusi-inspired form is a passageway where twigs and cut logs are meticulously stacked. A single clay urn stationed on top of the roof echoes the round red stones below.

the elements. Often, what has been discarded by man has already been subjected to the outdoors—in trash heaps and on roadsides—waiting to be carted away. The patina of age and weather actually enhances a found object's character; it can be left outdoors, not to litter but to improve with age.

Designer Mimi London uses rusted tin cans as outdoor spot lighting, the bulbs placed inside cans to illuminate specific trees in her yard. Artist Bill Shields displays old farm tools in the tiny garden of his San Francisco row house. Leftovers from his found art assemblages, these tools hang on fences and sit in the garden much to the surprise of guests who, says Shields, "delight at these objects peaking out at them."

Wood furniture—chairs, tables, chests—lacquered, varnished, or painted can be left outdoors to be bleached by the sun and smoothed by wind and rain. These pieces become part of their surroundings, as natural as the trees and stones and soil.

Nature bestows colors on found objects in the open air that distinguish them from domesticated materials. Wood bleaches to shades of blue and gray; metal takes on the burnt tones of autumn as it oxidates. Outdoors, natural and manmade objects exist in harmony, changing with the light from dawn to dusk.

Firewood wall, *near Mann's guest cottage, has the chunky texture of raw stone. In addition to providing a dependable supply of firewood, the wood stacks function as outdoor walls supported on either side by tree trunks or wooden posts. Whalebone supported on a frame of twigs leans against the wall at the end of the courtyard.*

Sand dollars and other shells *rest on a table formed of two rough chunks of wood. The bench and stool are formerly finished wood furniture that was left outside to be bleached and smoothed by the elements.*

Native rocks, *unearthed from the Mann/ Rosequist property, are clustered in a curve overlooking the Pacific. Covered with large canvas pillows, the rock formation becomes a comfortable and lavish outdoor seating area. Terra-cotta urns are turned upside down to serve as side tables.*

Weather-worn spool table *with all its imperfections is a humble stand for a quartet of perfectly shaped pots that emit musical sounds when the rain falls. The spindly forms that seem to grow from the pots in the background are twigs and sticks planted in a bed of sand and supported by white beach stones. The U-shaped pole is actually a metal topiary form.*

Serpentine driftwood *welcomes visitors to Ron Mann's guest cottage, a monastic dwelling in harmony with the natural elements. Leading to the curtained entrance are random chunks of wood—primitive forms that defy the turbulent winds and frequent changes in weather. A boat hatch, washed up on the beach, serves as the front stoop.*

Sculpture garden of found objects *reflects the originality of Ron Mann and Ivy Rosequist. This assembly of nature's artifacts appears in a stone-carpeted courtyard where a chaise longue and snack tables offer simple amenities.*

Railroad ties, *removed from an abandoned site, were used as landscape elements in a California backyard. In addition to warding off erosion, the logs blend with the wooded terrain, making an architectural terrace of the hillside. Pillars, steps, and even fencing are built from various lengths, each tie weathering at its own speed.*

Bone and twigs and sticks *are natural materials used outside a San Francisco home. The cattle skull, at left, a memento of a trip to the Mojave Desert, presents a jagged silhouette that appears to be part of the Pacific seascape. Twigs and sticks are wired together as primitive containers for succulents, at right.*

Sprawling tree trunk *provides ample seating when covered with throw pillows and acts as a table surface as well. Its crevices and contours are the handiwork of nature.*

Tree trunk fitted with a stone slab *is a corner pedestal in the same courtyard. The freeform trunk conforms to the height of a dining table.*

163

Sewer pipe *serves as a container for a potted palm placed inside its wide brim. Too bulky for most interiors, this roughhewn container is at home outdoors.*

Rusted tin can, *discarded by a California restaurant, was reclaimed to mask a spotlight that illuminates a palm tree. Pipes and hollowed-out logs can also be used as light shades.*

165

Saw blade, *which has been warped and oxidized by exposure to Colorado winters, looks like a caricature of the sun. Retired from active duty, the saw is suspended by heavy wire over a pile of wood cut by a different blade. Beneath the pitched overhang of a Vail ski house, this object has achieved new status as outdoor art.*

Logs and stones, *indigenous to the Colorado mountains, alternate to form a retaining wall. Large pieces of wood and rocks were recovered from the land while this hilltop home was being built. What might have been considered debris was used as natural building material to frame the rugged landscape.*

Assorted tools *hang on the barn siding of this Colorado ski house. No longer useful as working gear, the aging tools serve as an architectural detail on the snow-coated façade.*

Borders of stones *are used by food authority and restaurateur Robert Carrier as dividers between herbs and vegetables. This sprawling kitchen garden is located at Hintlesham Hall, Carrier's manor house in Suffolk, England.*

S AGENCY

Old plow, *discovered in an abandoned Kansas barn, was carted home to a San Francisco row house. The plow stands on top of a trellis in a vest-pocket garden, surrounded by smaller tools and spare auto parts.*

Bridge of logs *spans a river of stones in a typical Japanese-style garden. The hand-hewn bridge, made of matched twigs nailed to curved logs, could symbolize passing from the bustle of daily life into the tranquillity of a garden.*

Water-trough bar *is stocked for entertaining. The large metal trough, turned upside down, is an appropriate bar height; when not in use for that purpose, the metal stand is a showcase for bonsai plants. The remains of a rusted shovel hang on the fence like a piece of ancient art.*

Wire for hanging picture frames, *wound into circular forms, embellishes the cedar shingles of a California home. Illuminating the entranceway (at right angles to the wall) is another found object made of metal—a piece of stove pipe covering an unsightly light fixture. Standing to the right are large pieces of barnacle-encrusted driftwood found at the beach.*

Split logs, *gathered from a woodpile, form a perfect outdoor table for a sunny day in winter. When it begins to snow again, the logs can be returned to the pile or left under cover until spring.*

175

J. BARRY O'ROURKE

Small pieces of beach wood *have been assembled into a sculpture in the garden of Hubert Long's East Hampton home. The sculpture alters in the breeze, like the tiny branches of a tree.*

Large metal screw, *embedded in the frozen ground, resembles contemporary sculpture. The sharp-edged spiral cuts a striking form against the pure white background. Naked tree branches would be similarly effective on an open snow-field.*

177

Fire hose, *found in a derelict building, frames the original brass numerals on a converted building. In the process of turning the firehouse into living quarters, the owner painted the hose white, gilded both ends, and fastened it like a crest above the doorway.*

Top of fruit crate, *wired to a balcony rail, is a handy bird feeder. Its simple design is an unobtrusive part of the landscape and allows birds access from all sides.*

Split fire logs and a discarded cellar door *form an all-weather cocktail table on the deck of the Ruggiero home. The logs were fastened to the door with five-inch nails, original hinges and handle left in place so there is no mistaking its identity. Weathering with the rest of the found objects is an English bowling ball and a stack of plant flats used as a seat by daughter Meg.*

Log slices, *built up like a totem, stand outside the New England barn where they were found. Nailed together at each level, they are a steady series of platforms for flowering begonias.*

Paper-bag lights *hark back to Mexican luminarios. Facsimiles can be made with paper bags weighted with sand. Fill the bag up halfway, then fold back the top portion. Any thick candle can then be anchored in sand in the center of the bags. Plumbers' candles (found in hardware stores) burn longer than most decorative varieties.*

180

Material Possibilities

Where are found objects likely to be found? What to do with a bunch of twigs, a coconut shell, a terra-cotta flue pipe, a wood vegetable crate? Here is a comprehensive guide to objects and materials that can easily be adapted for use in and around the home.

The resources are arranged in alphabetical order in two sections— "From Nature" and "Man-Made." The entries provide a list of recommended sources with page numbers of the objects and materials as they appear in real-life settings. This guide is intended as a reference and inspiration for both the novice and the seasoned scavenger.

FROM NATURE

Bones and Horns

Sun-bleached skulls from the desert; horns and antlers from hunting trips or caches of trophies in attics, cellars, and garages; whalebones and fossils from the beach.

J. BARRY O'ROURKE

Branches

From forests, country roads, backyards, woodpiles, beaches.

Logs

From felled trees, nature trails, woodpiles.

Plants

From vegetable patches, flower gardens, the rural landscape.

NANCY NOVOGROD

Shells and Sea Forms

From beaches, riverbeds, personal collections.

JOSEPH RUGGIERO

NANCY NOVOGROD

Stones

From gardens, country roads, the rural landscape, riverbeds, beaches.

CHRIS MEAD

Tree Trunks

From backyards and country and suburban lots being cleared for new plantings and construction; lace-patterned cactus trunks from desert areas; bamboo from gardens and woodlands.

bamboo poles as ornaments, 138

MAN-MADE

Bottles and Bits of Glass

From kitchens, restaurants, beaches, vacant lots.

beach glass covering for tables and shelves, 127

MARGERY PETERS

Cans and Tins

From kitchens, restaurants, junkyards, dairies, garages.

RANDY O'ROURKE

Cardboard Boxes and Packaging

From supermarkets, liquor stores, kitchens, household discards.

MARGERY PETERS

Clothing, Sheets, and Rags

From castoffs and remnants in trunks, attics, closets, rag piles.

NANCY NOVOGROD

NANCY NOVOGROD

Metal Scraps and Equipment

From factory discards, junkyards, vacant lots, the street, warehouses, attics, cellars, garages.

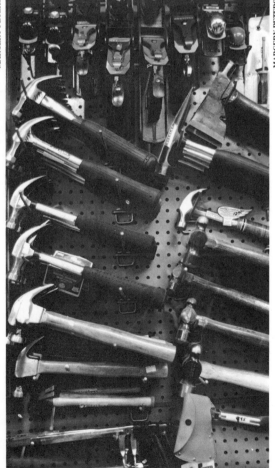

MARGERY PETERS

MARGERY PETERS

Paper Bags, Parchment, and Printed Matter

From rubbish piles, "junk" drawers, shopping trips; souvenirs.

JOSEPH RUGGIERO

Pipes, Spools, and Tubes

From junkyards, vacant lots, cellars; refuse at demolition and construction sites.

MARGERY PETERS

Plastic Cases and Containers

From filling stations, plant nurseries, vacant lots, kitchens; discarded household supplies.

J. BARRY O'ROURKE

Pottery

From garages, gardens, greenhouses, open markets.

RANDY O'ROURKE

Rubber

From vacant lots, junkyards, garages, cellars, kitchen cabinets, drawers.

Styrofoam Packing Material

From refuse at furniture, housewares, and appliance stores; vacant lots; discarded shipping molds.

MARGERY PETERS

Wire Baskets, Coils, Fencing, and Racks

From vacant lots, junkyards, farms, dairies, toolrooms, cellars, garages, beaches; refuse at construction sites.

MARGERY PETERS

Wood Baskets, Boxes, and Crates

From farms, vegetable stands, supermarkets, furniture and housewares stores, liquor stores, specialty shops for imported luxury food items.

JOSEPH RUGGIERO

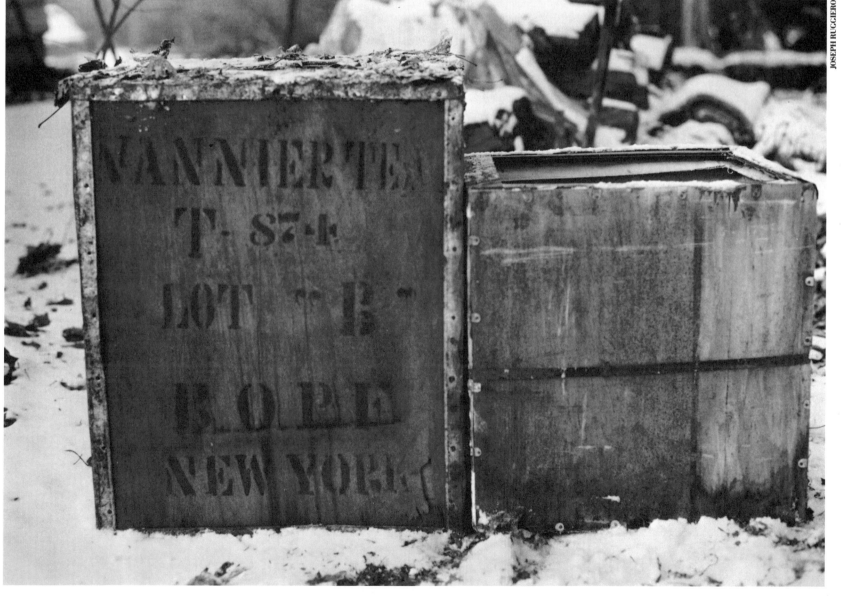

JOSEPH RUGGIERO

Wood Fragments and Furniture

From street demolition sites, junkyards, vacant lots, attics, cellars, garages, beaches.

J. BARRY O'ROURKE

Woven Grass and Straw Ropes

From attics, cellars, garages, beaches, boat basins; refuse from restaurants; grass mats used as packing material in some packages from the Far East.

DONA MEILACH

Index